A Thematic Catalog

of the Works

# of Robert Valentine

by

J. Bradford Young

MLA *Index and Bibliography Series*
Number 27

Canton, Massachusetts
Music Library Association, Inc.

Library of Congress Cataloging in Publication Data

Young, J. Bradford.
    A thematic catalog of the works of Robert Valentine / by J. Bradford Young.

        p.   cm. -- (MLA index and bibliography series, ISSN 0094-6478 ; no. 27)

        Includes bibliographical references.
        ISBN 0-914954-46-6

        1. Valentine, Robert, 1674-ca.1735--Thematic catalogs. I. Title. II. Series: MLA
index and bibliography series ; 27.

ML134.V27Y7 1994
016.78'092--dc20   94-4761
                                                                                    CIP
                                                                                    MN

MLA Index and Bibliography Series Number 27

ISBN: 0-914954-46-6
ISSN: 0094-6478

⊗ Printed on Acid-Free Paper by A-R Editions, Madison, Wisconsin 53717

A Thematic Catalog of the Works of Robert Valentine

MLA Index and Bibliography Series, Number 27
Deborah Campana, Editor

Individuals interested in submitting manuscripts for consideration in the series should correspond with the editor:

Deborah Campana
Music Library
Northwestern University
1935 Sheridan Road
Evanston, Illinois 60208-2300

to GGB for everything

Contents

PREFACE

Very little direct documentary evidence about Robert Valentine is known to exist, but what we do know has evolved primarily from a few manuscripts and numerous contemporary editions of his work. To gain a better understanding of this musician's work, I have studied these extant documents intending to identify their relationships and elucidate a context for their development. In making this study, it was essential to recognize the conditions of the production and distribution of his work because this information reflects the period in which Valentine lived. For example, although early eighteenth century musicians saw a great revival of music printing, both letterpress and engraved, much music was still copied in manuscript.[1]

Existing bibliographic information relating to Valentine's work is inadequate, primarily because the proliferation of engraved editions and their piracy have made it difficult to distinguish among publications. Many reference works are incomplete or incorrect in presenting as different editions of the same work, items containing different compositions, or in representing as different works, items containing the same composition. This problem has plagued all attempts to list Valentine's works. Much of the confusion also results from what evidently was Valentine's eastward migration; based upon the information presented in contemporary editions of his music, his career appears to have begun in the English provinces, and then progressed to Italy. To aid in analyzing these developments, the thematic catalog of the cousins Loelliet[2] was employed as a model. In the case of Valentine, however, it was necessary to reverse the process of sorting out different persons with similar names confused in the process of this migration.

The first objective of the present study was the resolution of these problems, because bibliographic work of this nature can only be undertaken with as complete as possible a knowledge of the composer's life and music. After identifying each work in Valentine's repertory, I compared the various manuscripts and published sources. The resultant product serves a twofold purpose: contributing toward the task of controlling the vast output of 18th century instrumental music and providing attributions for anonymous sources. I hope that my work will assist performers and librarians in identifying a substantial number of modern editions and recordings.

I would like to acknowledge the support and assistance of the staff at the University of Illinois Music Library, particularly William McClellan, and of Donald W. Krummel and Richard P. Smiraglia.

J. Bradford Young

1. H. Edmund Poole and Donald W. Krummel, "Printing and publishing of music. II: Publishing." *New Grove dictionary of music and musicians* (London: Macmillan, 1980) 15: 264.

2. Brian Priestman, "Catalogue thèmatique des oeuvres de Jean-Baptiste, John & Jacques Loelliet," *Revue belge de musicologie* 4, 4 (1952): 225-7, 258-69.

Editor's Note

The publication of this volume was facilitated by the contributions of a number of individuals. Foremost among them was Garrett Bowles, Music Librarian at University of California, LaJolla, who oversaw the digital encoding of the musical incipits. Without his help, it is doubtful that such a project could have been completed. I also appreciate the efforts of Melissa Jacobi and Vincent McCoy at the Northwestern University Library who provided advice on the technical apparatus available for this project, and of Ginger Kroft, student assistant at the Northwestern University Music Library, who assisted with proofreading and in making typographical changes.

Deborah Campana
Editor, MLA Index and Bibliography Series

INTRODUCTION TO CATALOG

All manifestations of each work in Valentine's repertory are identified and described according to the standards indicated below. All extant works have been included, and no attempt has been made to identify anonymous works not previously attributed to him. Manuscripts and editions unavailable for inspection have been described from published sources. Original works are cited first (including those in multiple versions), followed by contemporary arrangements and fragments.

Mere transpositions are not considered different works. In some cases, however, the same upper part serves solo, duet and trio versions, and these relationships are noted. Some of these were published in duet and trio versions with identical upper parts. The duets have been treated as contemporary arrangements.

Each numbered entry represents one of Valentine's works, often as many as twelve sonatas published as a set. The original title of each is given as well as the place and date of its first publication, when known. A statement of genre, medium and key, or sequence of keys, follows. Annotations of additional versions of a work are given as applicable. Detailed descriptions of the early editions precede brief listings of manuscripts, modern editions and recordings.

Early editions are described in some detail because they provide the central source of information regarding Valentine's life and work. No attempt was made to formulate the ideal copy as in an analytical bibliography. Each description was prepared from a single copy. Analysis of content is provided for incomplete editions, or for those in which the order varies from that of the incipit. The publisher's name appears with the date of impression; when possible, a missing date has been supplied from an external source. Publisher numbers are provided along with a brief physical description identifying format and printing process used.

The next item is a title page transcription: quasi-facsimile for letter-press editions or a simplified form for engraved editions. Only a few were printed from movable type. No standard exists for the description of engraved music. Because it was not feasible to provide the reproductions Fredson Bowers and others consider neccessary,[1] and sophisticated quasi-facsimile transcriptions are not adequate substitutes, a simplified form outlined by Bowers has been used.[2]

When present, dedicatory pages are also transcribed. Annotations include the repository and shelfmark of the exemplar described, a register of other known copies, the source of an externally supplied date, contemporary references, citations for published descriptions and other various notes as needed.

After analysis of the content for those which are incomplete, the description of manuscripts is limited to the repository, shelfmark and foliation, transcription of title information and brief physical description. Information about the provenance is supplied when possible from published sources. Annotations of other published descriptions and any other notes follow; hopefully, these descriptions will aid the user in locating the manuscript.

Modern editions and sound recordings are described as briefly as possible, providing only enough detail to identify them. This includes content analysis for incomplete items, indication of arrangement, title proper, statements of responsibility (other than the composer), imprint and publisher's, or manufacturer's number. Series statements and standard numerical designations are included when possible to expedite library retrieval. Principal performers are named for recordings.

The disposition of individual sonatas within a set varies among sources, as does the opus numbering found in the early editions. The Walsh editions have been used as a paradigm for the group of items within numbered sets, because they form the most comprehensive uniformly numbered sources. Thematic incipits are given in score from the Walsh or other earliest edition or, if unpublished, from the manuscript.

1. *Principles of bibliographic description* (New York: Russell & Russell, 1962), 178.

2. Ibid., 138.

BIOGRAPHY OF ROBERT VALENTINE

NATIONALITY

The name, Robert Valentine, has come down to us through contemporary editions of his works. The earliest of these were published in Italy and refer to him as Roberto Valentine. Despite occasional appearances of an Italian form of his surname, Valentini or Valentino, the sobriquent, Inglese, is generally associated with his name, suggesting English nationality. Subsequent London editions of the same works state on the title page, "composed by Mr. Valentine at Rome." The 1708 edition of his opus 2 recorder sonatas published in Rome by Mascardi[1] is the earliest extant edition of any work by Valentine. In it appears a dedication to Sir Thomas Samwell, indicating that the young Englishman may have been Robert Valentine's patron. New works attributed to Roberto Valentine Inglese or "composed by Mr. Valentine at Rome," continue to appear in print throughout the following twenty-five years. In sum, these facts point to a composer living in Italy, who was probably born in England around 1675.

Four reference works published in the eighteenth century mention Valentine's works. Johann Gottfried Walther in his *Musikalisches Lexikon*[2] (1732) lists those issued by the Amsterdam publisher, Roger, under an entry for Roberto Valentine. The German form of his name, Robert Valentin, heads an article reprinted nearly verbatim in the *Grosses vollständiges Universal-Lexikon* published by Johann Heinrich Zedler[3] (1745). Both Charles Burney and Sir John Hawkins referred briefly to Valentine in their histories (1776): in discussing the popularity of the recorder earlier in the century, Hawkins refers to the solos of "Robert Valentine of Rome,"[4] whereas Burney, in a comment on the music made available by the London publisher John Walsh in 1733, includes flute solos by a "Valentini,"[5] which the Walsh bibliography reveals as Robert Valentine.[6] None of the four references suggests that Valentine was English, however.

The first published statement identifying Robert Valentine as English appeared in Ernst Ludwig Gerber's *Neues historisch-biographisches Lexikon der Tonkünstler*[7] (1812-1813). His entry, "Robert Valentini," is another reprint of Walther's list of Roger editions, here ascribed to an English instrumentalist who lived around 1720. The *Cyclopaedia*[8] (1819) edited by

Abraham Rees states that Roberto Valentini was "an Englishman, a voluminous composer for the common flute, whose works were chiefly published by Roger at Amsterdam." It should be noted that Charles Burney spent the last years of his life writing articles for this encyclopedia; the main contributor on music, he may have written this entry, as its emphasis on the recorder and the Roger editions are consistent with earlier data. James Duff Brown included Robert Valentine in his British musical biography[9] (1897), however John Alexander Fuller-Maitland's article written for *Grove's dictionary of music and musicians*[10] described him as English or Italian.

FAMILY

Percy Young, in his article for *Die Musik in Geschichte und Gegenwart* was the first to trace a connection from Robert Valentine to a family of Valentines[11] who were active in England throughout the eighteenth century. He discovered that Thomas Follintine, of the city of Leicester, was the progenitor of four generations of musical Valentines, as the family name came to be known. Young thought that Robert was perhaps his grandson but found no date of birth. Martin Medforth provided further details about Robert Valentine's origins, culled from baptismal records: Robert Valentine was christened on January 16, 1673 (old style) in St. Martin's church, the fourth son of Thomas Follintine and his wife Sarah.[12]

Thomas Follintine was entered in the Freemen's Register for the Borough of Leicester on April 2, 1684. Martin Medforth believes he arrived around 1670 to take a job as one of the town musicians.[13] Robert is among the ten children to whom reference is made in his father's will of February 13, 1684/5.[14] Robert Valentine's two older brothers were among the four new waits appointed by the Leicester Borough Council in 1685. On New Year's Day 1696/7 the council "ordered then that the waites shall be discharged and their badges and cloakes taken from them."[15] Henry continued to be active as a musician. Medforth states that he was organist at St. Martin's Church as early as 1701. The Freemen's Register records David Langron who received his freedom on January 31, 1721/2 as "an apprentice of Henry Volentine of Leicester, organist."[16]

The second brother, Thomas, had received the freedom, probably as a hosier, three years before the waits were discharged. That he continued to be involved musically is borne out by his will, which describes him as a musician.[17] Six of Thomas' sons became professional musicians. In fact, his brother Henry was succeeded as organist at St. Martin's Church by one of his sons, also named Henry. Thomas' grandson John was widely known in England as a composer and was active in Leicester as a music seller, performer and concert organizer.

In 1762 John Valentine and his cousin Henry, also a grandson of Thomas Valentine, arranged a series of subscription concerts.[18] In 1785 another concert series began under John and his daughter Ann; Henry and his children, Fanny and Robert.[19] The members of the Valentine family, the only professional musicians involved in the concerts, earned their living by assisting with such affairs.

ROME

The reference to Robert Valentine in his father's will, drawn up in Leicester in 1685 when Robert was eleven, is the last evidence of his life in England. In eighteenth-century English sources his name is closely associated with Rome;[20] as noted earlier, virtually all his London editions credit "Mr. Valentine living in Rome" or "Mr. Valentine at Rome,"[21] and many of his compositions were first published in Rome.[22] These works, approximately one dozen sets of sonatas, provide the first documentation of his adult life and copies are extant for about half.

According to RISM Series A I, no copy of the Roman edition of his first published work, the opus 1 trio sonatas is extant. It must date from before his 1708 opus 2 recorder sonatas.[23] In 1710 Vitale Mascardi published another set, opus 3 recorder sonatas, and the following year, the trio sonatas opus 4 for violin entitled *Balletti da camera*.[24] These were all printed from movable type and carry the customary imprint that provides the date. Sonatas opera 5 and 6 were printed in Italy from engraved plates, and as was usual for this type of printing, no imprint dates were included. Based on the date of the Amsterdam and London reprints a probable date of publication between 1712 and 1715 can be assigned to the Italian editions. There is no more evidence of his works being published in Italy until around 1730 when Antonio Cleton published the opus 12 flute sonatas.[25] The last was the violin sonatas op. 13, *La villegiatura*.[26] The corresponding gap in the dates of publication and the sequence of opus numbers suggests that five other works, for which copies are not extant, were printed. These survive only in English editions which may be reprints of Italian sources.

In the same years that his compositions were first published, Robert Valentine was employed as a performer by the Marquis Francesco Maria Ruspoli. George Frideric Handel composed several works for Ruspoli during his own Italian journeys. *La resurrezione* was first performed on Easter 1708 at the Palazzo Bonelli under the direction of Arcangelo Corelli,[27] as Ursula Kirkendale has has documented from the Ruspoli court account books.[28] Cited as serving among the extra musicians was an oboist named Valentini, who Martin Medforth believes was Robert Valentine because no other oboists of that name were known to have been active in Rome at this time.[29] The following year Antonio Caldara began his tenure as maestro di capella to Ruspoli. Under him the oboist Valentini appears in the accounts published by

Kirkendale for August 27, 1709 and March 16, 1710.[30] There is no direct evidence concerning how or why Robert Valentine came to be in Italy. Speculation on these questions is difficult because nothing is known about his life between birth and his first documented activity in Rome. Although it is doubtful that a person of provincial background would make a journey to the Continent unassisted, without an opportunity as a wait, Valentine may have left Leicester to seek employment elsewhere. Or, an English patron may have taken him to Italy; at this time it was customary for Englishmen to take journeys through Europe that could last for years, and Valentine may have been part of the retinue accompanying such a tour.

Percy Young has suggested that one such patron might have been Sir Thomas Samwell, to whom Valentine dedicated his opus 2 recorder sonatas.[31] Samwell (1687-1757), a landowner from Upton in Northamptonshire, was interested in music and art and toured Europe extensively. He owned a portrait of Pierre Bufardin, a flute virtuoso at Dresden.[32] He attended Cambridge University in 1704, and then in 1707 departed on a long tour of Europe to complete his education.[33] It is possible that Valentine might have been considered an appropriate musical guide for the young amateur on his journey. It is not known just when Samwell returned to England, but it would probably have been prior to 1715, when he was elected a Member of Parliament for Conventry.[34] This time frame, in fact, corresponds with the gap in the Italian publication schedule of Valentine's compositions. Martin Medforth argues, however, that Valentine must have gone to Rome before Samwell's tour,[35] because by the spring of 1708, he had composed a set of trio sonatas which reveal a greater understanding of Corelli's style than he could have gained in England. Moreover, Valentine had been accepted as a performer at the Ruspoli court, one of Rome's most prestigious musical institutions. Had he arrived in 1707, a rapid assimilation into Italian musical life would have to have been made. The dedication to Samwell of Valentine's opus 2 sonatas may have been merely the result of their meeting in Rome.

An often-cited claim that Robert Valentine was in Rome during March of 1714 is based upon a letter by Pietro Locatelli dated March 17, 1714. In it, Locatelli describes an unidentified "Valentini."[36] Giovanni Simone Mayr refers to Locatelli's return to Rome at this time "in compagno di certo Valentini suo grand'amico."[37] Antonio Alessandri further annotates this passage with an abridged quotation of the letter which refers to "Valentino,"[38] identifying the companion, in a footnote, as a famous flautist, who returned to London in 1731, thereby suggesting Robert Valentine.[39] Most subsequent works repeat Alessandri's information in reference to Robert Valentine with or without a citation to the source. Michael Talbot considers the letter to be evidence that Locatelli studied with Giuseppe Valentini rather than Arcangelo Corelli,[40] which would refute Alessandri's identification.[41]

MATURITY

Robert Valentine may have left Rome to pursue his career in other cities. Percy Young speculates that Valentine had an acquaintance with early eighteenth-century North German composers for the flute, based on the unique manuscript copies of Valentine's compositions in Northern repositories such as Hannover, Rostock and Uppsala.[42] Because Thomas Samwell owned a portrait of Pierre Buffardin, Young suggests he may have visited Dresden on his European tour and taken Valentine with him. Martin Medforth believes that his suggestion is not supported by the evidence.[43] Valentine's dedication to another patron in 1710 implies that he was no longer under Samwell's patronage, and there would have been few opportunities for Samwell and Valentine to have visited Dresden together.

It is possible that Robert Valentine worked in Naples, based on the fact that his employment at the Ruspoli court places him there in 1710. In that year his opus 3 recorder sonatas were published at Rome with a dedication to John Fleetwood, British consul at Naples.[44] Though it is not clear that Valentine was under Fleetwood's patronage, it is known that Fleetwood became a Member of Parliament in 1713.[45] Further evidence of Valentine's possible connections to Naples dates from fifteen or twenty years later. The library of the Conservatorio di San Pietro a Majella in Naples preserves a set of manuscript parts copied around 1725, that contain concertos for recorder and strings by various composers known to have been active in Naples at that time.[46] Included is a work in B-flat attributed to Roberto Valentini. Its style is by no means inconsistent with his published works, and Martin Medforth finds similarities between this concerto and the opus 12 flute sonatas, suggesting they were composed at about the same time.[47] The opus 12 sonatas were published in 1740, by Antonio Cleton, and the dedicatee was Gennaro Moccia, a duke of the Kingdom of Naples.

Evidence links Robert Valentine less directly with other major Italian music centers. His *Divertimento a due flauti* published around 1715 is dedicated to the Grand Prince Gian Gastone de'Medici, later Grand Duke of Tuscany.[48] Gian Gastone had met Handel in Hamburg and invited him to visit Florence, where he was very generous.[49] Valentine may have come in contact with the Prince through the Ruspoli court. Two manuscripts containing recorder music by Robert Valentine are in the Biblioteca palatina in Parma, among a great many manuscripts of eighteenth-century chamber music.[50] The dates for these items are not known but the contents suggest the 1720's. The opus 11 recorder sonatas contained in one manuscript are not known to have been published in Italy, but appeared in London in 1727.[51] The other manuscript contains eighteen sonatas for one and two recorders with continuo. None of his trio sonatas for recorder are known to have been published until the London editions of 1718-1721.[52] These manuscripts probably originate in the same period as does that at Naples.

RETURN TO ENGLAND

It is not known if Robert Valentine ever returned to England. Though it has been suggested that he returned to London in 1731, the origin of this information seems to be the 1875 footnote to the Locatelli anecdote mentioned above.[53] Alessandri's footnote with uncertainty identifies the Valentini in question as a famous flautist who published various works for that instrument in Amsterdam.[54] It seems clear that Alessandri was referring to Robert Valentine, without giving the name, although Locatelli probably was not. Alessandri states that in 1731, this same person was in London, although no source for this information is given, and it cannot be accounted for in any way, though it has been repeated in several reference works.[55]

The only other clues regarding Robert Valentine's possible return to England lie in the chronology of his published works. By tracing the patterns between English and Continental editions, some speculations can be supported. A return around 1731, mentioned by Alessandri is confirmed by some bibliographic data. The firm of Walsh and Hare issued a dozen of Valentine's compositions between 1712 and 1730, and around that time they were all reissued.[56] This was a period of transition for the firm, with the younger John Walsh assuming control of the business, succeeding his father in May 1731. The relationship with the Hare family ended about the same time.[57] The apparent reissue of all Valentine's works might have been due entirely to the publisher's internal policies.

Of Valentine's compositions published in Italy before 1730, only the *Balletti da camera* (1711) were never published in England. In fact, the only works published in England after 1730 were the opus 12 violin sonatas, opus 13 flute sonatas and opus 14 flute duets, which are *not* the works published in Italy as opus 12 and 13. These three were never published in Europe. The earliest extant Italian editions of Valentine from 1708 and 1710 are dedicated to Englishmen, that of 1730 is dedicated to a Neapolitan Duke. The Roman edition of opus 13 is dedicated to Sir George Pitt, the first English dedicatee in the twenty preceding years. Pitt had been a Member of Parliament for nearly thirty years, losing his seat in 1722, before his death in 1734.[58] The drastic change in publication pattern around 1730 or 1731 seems to indicate that a change in Valentine's career had taken place.

PUBLICATION PATTERNS

Bibliographical evidence points to parallels between Robert Valentine's career and publishing history. The contemporary editions comprise four periods, each with its own characteristic pattern of publication. The first extends circa 1708 to 1715, defined by the six works published in Rome. Each of these was reprinted in Amsterdam one or two years later by Etienne Roger, who "pirated" a great many Italian editions at this time. These were sold in many different cities including London. There the Roger editions themselves were pirated by John Walsh,[59] who, between 1712 and 1714, issued the first three of Valentine's Roman publications.[60] This pattern strongly suggests that Valentine lived in Italy at this time.

The next period ranges from 1715 to 1721, when no new works are known to have been published in Europe, while at least a dozen new editions appeared in London. In 1715 only the first three of the six works previously published had appeared in London. Walsh published in 1715 a version of the *Divertimento a due flauti* just published in Rome.[61] In 1718, Walsh published the opus 5 recorder sonatas. The first six of these correspond to those published in Rome and Amsterdam as "opera quinta parte prima."[62] By 1720, Walsh published two more sets of duets for recorder, opera 6 and 7.[63] His opus 6 includes a sonata from the *Divertimento a due flauti* which had been omitted from his publication of opus 4. Also included are four of the opus 3 recorder sonatas arranged as duets. There were other arrangements as well. The sonatas opera 4 and 7 were published for two violins. Daniel Wright issued versions of both the opera 4 and 6 recorder duets as trio sonatas for violin. The imprint of the first of these reads "printed for the author at the Old Post office in Rusel (sic) Street, Covent Garden." Later impressions read "Compo'd by Mr. Valentine, living at Rome, and printed by Daniel Wright, musical instrument maker, next to the Sun Tavern in Holborn." The British Library catalogue dates this edition around 1715.[64] Wright's later publications from this period drop the phrase "living at Rome" from Valentine's name. Walsh maintains the form "comp'sed by Mr. Valentine at Rome" consistently perhaps because he reused the engraved title page with slight modification for several works. In addition to the duet and trio arrangements that had not been published in Europe, three sets of trio-sonatas for recorder, titled *Setts of aires*, were published for the first time in London between 1718 and 1721.[65] The appearance of so many new works, many in multiple versions, editions and issues, in the space of only six years following an equally sudden break in the previously regular pattern of publication suggests a change of some sort around 1715. Samwell and Fleetwood would both have returned to England by this time. Perhaps Valentine found himself without patronage in Italy and also returned.

From 1721 to 1727, the publication of Robert Valentine's works came to a sudden stop. During the previous fifteen years an average of two editions a year had been issued, but following the publication of the opus 10 trio sonatas in 1721, nothing was published for six years, until the opus 11 recorder sonatas were published by Walsh in 1727.[66] The publication of Valentine's music could have halted during this period because he was composing works inappropriate for publication. His compositions published before 1722, were appropriate for amateurs, as was most music published at this time. It was among the great body of amateur musicians that publishers found their market. Professional musicians did not provide as lucrative a return. They were also very protective of their own repertories and did not wish to share them by publication. Orchestral parts would not have been printed if it were not for the amateur musical societies. For this reason manuscript was the medium of dissemination for professionals while print was for amateurs. By this time Valentine may have achieved a reputation as a soloist, and could have supported himself through paid appearances in professional orchestral performances. It would follow that his compositional activities at this time might support his work as a performer, if he produced concertos rather than simple duets. These professionally-oriented compositions are less likely to have been published and less likely to have survived. Those that have been found, exist only in manuscript and are quite different from the published works of the first two periods. The few surviving manuscripts are of Italian provenance, suggesting that if Valentine did establish a career as a professional performer it was in Italy.

In the final period of publication, 1727-1747, several new works were published and earlier works reprinted, thus reinforcing the idea that Robert Valentine had established a career as a professional performer by this time. The opus 11 recorder sonatas published by Walsh in 1727, are his last works for the recorder.[67] By this time professionals had long favored the flute.[68] In the next year Walsh brought out the idiomatic opus 12 violin sonatas, Valentine's first solo composition for that instrument.[69] Two years later a set of flute sonatas dated 1730 was published at Rome by Antonio Cleton,[70] the first new European edition of his works in fifteen years. Antonio Cleton also published at Rome *La villeggiatura*, dedicated to Sir George Pitt[71]; this edition is not dated but have followed the work of 1730, but preceded the death of Sir George in 1734.[72]

In 1735, the younger John Walsh published the opus 13 flute sonatas.[73] He had recently reprinted all twelve of Valentine's works previously published by his father.[74] These are all listed for sale on the title page of opus 13.[75] At about this time, Parisian music publishers were greatly increasing their production, and several of Valentine's earlier works were reprinted there around 1740.[76] Robert Valentine's last published composition, the opus 14 flute duets, was included in a collection published by Walsh around 1747.[77] The collection featured works by Hasse, Handel, Arne, Boyce and other composers who were well known in England, but all younger than Valentine,[78] who would have been in his seventies. This publication might be posthumous, since twelve years had elapsed between the publication of opus 13 and opus 14.

Notes

1.   Karlheinz Schlager, ed. *Einzeldrucke vor 1800*. Répertoire international des sources musicales. Série A I. (Kassel: Barenreiter, 1971-1983) 9: 4 (V5O).

2.   Johann Gottfried Walther, *Musikalisches Lexikon* (Leipzig: Wolffgang Deer, 1732), 624.

3.   "Robert Valentine," In *Grosses vollständiges Universal-Lexikon aller Wissenschaften und Künste...* vol. 46 (Leipzig: Johann Heinrich Zedler, 1745), 227.

4.   John Hawkins, *A general history of the science and practice of music*, vol. 2 (1853; reprint, New York: Dover, 1963), 738.

5.   Charles Burney, *A general history of music from the earliest times to the present period*, vol.2 (1789; reprint, New York: Dover, 1957), 1003.

6.   William C. Smith and Charles Humphries, *A bibliography of the musical works published by the firm of John Walsh during the years 1721-1766* (London: The Bibliographical Society, 1968), 328-32.

7.   Ernst Ludwig Gerber, *Neues Historisch-Biographisches Lexikon der Tonkunstler*, vol.2 (Leipzig: A.Kuhnel, 1812-14), 421.

8.   "Robert Valentini," *The Cyclopaedia, or, Universal Dictionary of Arts, Sciences, and Literature*, by Abraham Rees, vol. 36 (Philadelphia: Bradford, Murray, Fairman, 1819), v.d.

9.   James Duff Brown, *British Musical Biography, a Dictionary of Musical Artists, Authors, and Composers Born in Britain and its Colonies*, by James D. Brown...and Stephen S. Stratton (Birmingham: S.S.Stratton, 1897), 422.

10.   John Alexander Fuller-Maitland, "Robert Valentine," vol.8, *Grove's dictionary of music and musicians*, 5th ed. (London: Macmillan, 1954), 652-53.

11.   Percy M. Young, "Robert Valentine," *Die Musik in Geschichte und Gegenwart* (Kassel: Barenreiter, 1966), 13: 1226-28.

12.   Martin Medforth, "The Valentines of Leicester," *Musical Times* 122 (December 1981), 812-18.

13.   Ibid., 813.

14.   Ibid., 813.

15   G. A. Chinnery, ed., *Records of borough of Leicester*. Hall books and papers 1689-1835, New series, Vol. 5 (Leicester: E. Backus, 1965), 21 (item 58).

16.   Henry Hartopp, ed., *Register of the freemen of Leicester: Records of the borough of Leicester*, New series, vols. 1-2 (Leicester: E. Backus, 1927-33), 1: 246.

17.   Medforth, "Valentines," 815. Citation to Leicester Record Office Will no,. 261.

18.   James Thompson, *The history of Leicester in the eighteenth century*. History of Leicester, vol.2. (Leicester: Crossley & Clark, 1871), 111.

19.   William Gardiner, *Music and friends; or Pleasant Recollections of a Dilettante*, 3 vols.(London: Longman et al, 1838-53), 1: 67.

20.   Hawkins, *History*, 2: 738.

21.   Smith and Humphries, *Walsh*, 328-32.

22.   RISM A I, 9: 4-6.

23.   Ibid., 4 (V50).

24.   Ibid., 4 (V50).

25.   Ibid., 6 (V80).

26.   Ibid., 6 (V84).

27.   Hans Joachim Marx, "Francesco Maria Ruspoli," *The New Grove Dictionary of Music and Musicians* (London: Macmillan, 1980) 16: 334.

28.   Ursula Kirkendale, "The Ruspoli documents on Handel," *Journal of the American Musicological Society* 20, 2 (April 1967), 256 (document 11).

29.   Medforth, "Valentines," 813.

30.   Ursula Kirkendale, *Antonio Caldara: sein Leben und seine venezianisch-römischen oratorien*. Wiener Musikwissenschaftliche Beiträge, Bd.6. (Graz: Böhlaus, 1966), 355, 358, 361.

31.   Young, "Robert Valentine," 1226.

32.   Ibid.

33.   John Venn, comp., *Alumni Cantabrigiensis*, 10 vols. (Cambridge, England: The University Press, 1922-54), Part 1,4: 12.

34.   Ibid.

35.   Medforth, "Valentines," 813.

36.   Ibid., 815.

37.   Giovanni Simone Mayr, *Biografie di scrittori e artisti musicali bergamaschi nativi od Oriundi* (Bergamo: Pagnoncelli, 1875), 89.

38.   Ibid., 177.

39.   Ibid., 89.

40.   Arend Koole and Michael Talbot, "Pietro Antonio Locatelli," *The New Grove Dictionary of Music and Musicians*, 11: 104.

41.   Medforth, "Valentines," 815.

42.   Percy M. Young, *A History of British music* (New York: W.W. Norton, 1967), 372 n. 2.

43.   Medforth, "Valentines," 815 n. 12.

44.   RISM A I, 9: 4 (V 56).

45.   Joseph Foster, ed., *Alumni Oxonienses...* Series 1 (4 vols.): 1500-1714, (Oxford: James Parker & Co., 1891-92), 2: 506.

46.   Associazione di Musicologi Italiani. *Catalogo delle opere musicali teoriche e pratiche...: Città di Napoli. Biblioteca del R. Conservatorio di musica di S. Pietro a Majella... .* Series 10. Compiled by Guido Gasperini e Franca Gallo (Parma: Freschi, 1934), 2: 548.

47.   Medforth, "Valentines," 815.

48.   RISM A I, 9: 5 (V70).

49.   Frank A. D'Accone, "Medici," *The New Grove Dictionary of Music and Musicians*, 12: 14.

50.   Associazione dei Musicologi Italiani. *Catalogo generale delle opere musicali, teoriche o pratiche... Città di Parma.* Compiled by Guido Gasperini and Nestore Pellicelli (Parma: Zerbini & Freschig, 1911),259.

51.   Smith and Humphries, *Walsh*, 331 (#1490).

52.   Edith B. Schnapper, ed. *British Union Catalogue of Early Music Printed Before the Year 1980.*

2 vols. (London: Butterworths Scientific Publications, 1957), 2: 1032.

53.   Mayr, *Biografie*, 89.

54.   Ibid., 89. Note: "Non osiamo di asseriere, benctie ci sembra probabile, che questi fosse quel celebrato suonatore di flauto, che nel 1731 trovavasi a Londra, e fece stampare in Amsterdam varie opere per quell'istromento."

55.   Medforth, "Valentines," 815.

56.   Smith and Humphries, *Walsh*, 328-32.

57.   Frank Kidson, William C. Smith and Peter Ward Jones, "John Walsh (ii)," *The New Grove Dictionary of Music and Musicians*, 20: 186.

58.   Foster, *Alumni*, 3: 1169.

59.   Samuel F. Pogue, "Estienne Roger," *The New Grove Dictionary of Music and Musicians*, 16: 99-100.

60.   François Lesure, *Bibliographie des Éditions musicales publiées par Estienne Roger et Michel-Charles Le Cene*. Publications de la Société française de musicologie, series 2, vol. 12 (Paris: Société française de musicologie, Heugel et Cie., 1969), 83.

61.   William C. Smith, *A bibliography of musical works published by John Walsh during the years 1695-1720* (London: Printed for the Bibliographical Society at the University Press, Oxford 1948).

62.   Ibid., 158 (#554).

63.   Ibid., 162-63 (#572, 575)

64.   W. Barclay Squire, *Catalogue of printed music published between 1487-1800 now in the British Museum*. 2 vols. (London: Printed by order of the Trustees, 1912), 2: 614.

65.   Smith, *Walsh*, 158 (#552); Smith and Humphries, *Walsh*, 328-29 (#1476, 1478).

66.   Smith and Humphries, *Walsh*, 331 (#1490).

67.   Ibid.

68.   David Lasocki, "Professional recorder playing in England 1500-1740. II: 1640-1740," *Early Music* 20, 2 (April 1982), 191.

69.   Smith and Humphries, *Walsh*, 331-32 (#1492).

70.   RISM A I, 9: 11 (V80).

71.   Ibid., 11 (V84).

72.   Foster, *Alumni*, 3: 1169.

73.   Smith and Humphries, *Walsh*, 332 (#1494).

74.   Ibid., 228-32.

75.   Smith and Humphries, *Walsh*, 332 (#1494).

76.   Anik Devriès and François Lesure, *Des origines à environ 1820. Dictionnaire des editeurs de musique français*, vol.1 (Genèva: Éditions Minkoff, 1979), 263.

77.   Smith and Humphries, *Walsh*, 121-22 (#553).

78.   François Lesure, ed., *Recueils imprimés XVIIIe siècle.* Répertoire International des Sources Musicales. Serie B II (Munich: G.Henle Verlag, 1964), 199.

BIBLIOGRAPHY

Associazione dei Musicologi Italiani. *Catalogo delle opere musicali teoriche e pratiche...: Città di Napoli. Biblioteca del R. Conservatorio di musica di S. Pietro a Majella... .* Compiled by Guido Gasperini e Franca Gallo. Parma: Freschig, 1934. (Cited as Gasperini (Naples))

Associazione dei Musicologi Italiani. *Catalogo generale delle opere musicali, teoriche o pratiche... Città di Parma.* Compiled by Guido Gasperini and Nestore Pellicelli. Parma: Zerbini & Fresching, 1911. (Cited as Gasperini (Parma))

Bittmann, Inge, comp. *Catalogue of Giedde's Music Collection in the Royal Library of Copenhagen.* [Egtved]: Edition Egtved, 1976. (Cited as Giedde)

Bodemann, Eduard, ed. *Die Handschriften der Königlichen öffentlichen bibliothek zu Hannover.* Hannover: Hahn, 1867. (Cited as Bodemann)

Brown, James Duff. *British Musical Biography, a Dictionary of Musical Artists, Authors, and Composers Born in Britain and its Colonies,* by James D. Brown ... and Stephen S. Stratton. Birmingham: S.S.Stratton, 1897.

Burney, Charles. *A General History of Music, from the Earliest Times to the Present Period.* 4 books. London: Printed for the author, 1789. Reprint ed. with critical and historical notes by Frank Mercer. (4 books in 2 volumes) New York: Dover Publications, 1957.

Chinnery, G.A., ed. *Records of Borough of Leicester.* Hall books and papers 1689-1835, new series, vol. 5. Leicester: E.Backus, 1965.

D'Accone, Frank A. "Medici." In *The New Grove Dictionary of Music and Musicians* 12: 13-15. London: Macmillan, 1980.

Devriès, Anik and François Lesure. *Des Origines à Environ 1820.* Dictionnaire des Editeurs de Musique Français, vol. 1. Genève: Éditions Minkoff, 1979.

Écorcheville, J. *Catalogue du Fonds de Musique Ancienne de la Bibliothèque Nationale.* 8 vols. Société internationale de musique. Paris: J. Terquem, 1910-1914. Reprint. New York: Da Capo Press, 1972. (Cited as Écorcheville).

Edwards, Owain. "The response to Corelli's music in eighteenth-century England." *Studia Musicologica Norvegica* 2 (1976): 51-96.

Eitner, Robert. *Biographisch-Bibliographisches Quellen-Lexikon der Musiker und Musikgelehrten der christlichen Zeitrechnung bis zur Mitte des Neunzehnten Jahrhunderts.* 10 vols. Leipzig: Breitkopf & Härtel, 1898-1904. Reprint. New York: Musurgia, [1947]. (Cited as Eitner)

Fiske, Roger. *English Theatre Music in the Eighteenth-Century.* London: Oxford University Press, 1973.

Foster, Joseph, ed. *Alumni Oxonienses: The Members of the University of Oxford; Their Parentage, Birthplace and Year of Birth, with a Record of their Degrees. Being the matriculation register of the University, alphabetically arranged, revised and annotated.* Series 1 (4 vols.): 1500-1714. Oxford: James Parker & Co., 1891-92.

Fuller-Maitland, John Alexander. "Robert Valentine." In *Grove's Dictionary of Music and Musicians.* 5th edition. Vol. 8, 652-653. London: Macmillan, 1954.

Gardiner, William. *Music and Friends; or, Pleasant Recollections of a Dilettante.* 3 vols. London: Longman, 1838-1853.

Gerber, Ernst Ludwig. *Neues Historisch-Biographisches Lexikon der Tonkünstler.* [supplement to his *Historisch-Biographisches Lexicon de Tonkünstler*] Leipzig: A. Kuhnel, 1812-14.

Hartopp, Henry, ed. *Register of the Freemen of Leicester: Records of the Borough of Leicester.* New series, vols. 1-2. Leicester: E.Backus, 1927-1933.

Hawkins, John, Sir. *A General History of the Science and Practice of Music.* 2 vols. London: J.A.Novello, 1853. Reprint, with a new introduction by Charles Cudworth. New York: Dover Publications, <1963>.

Hopkinson, Cecil. *A Dictionary of Parisian Music Publishers 1700-1950.* London: Printed for the author, 1954.

Hughes-Hughes, Augustus. *Catalogue of Manuscript Music in the British Museum.* 3 vols. London: Printed by order of the trustees, 1906-1909.

Kidson, Frank; William C. Smith; and Peter Ward Jones. "John Walsh (ii)." *The New Grove Dictionary of Music and Musicians* 20: 186. London: Macmillan, 1980.

Kirkendale, Ursula. *Antonio Caldara: sein Leben und seine venezianisch-römischen oratorien.* Wiener Musikwissenschaftliche Beiträge Bd.6. Graz; Köln: Hermann Böhlaus, 1966.

Kirkendale, Ursula. "The Ruspoli documents on Handel." *Journal of the American Musicological Society* 20, 2 (April 1967): 222-273.

Koole, Arend and Michael Talbot. "Pietro Antonio Locatelli." In *The New Grove Dictionary of Music* and Musicians 11: 104-107. London: Macmillan, 1980.

Krummel, D.W., ed. *Bibliographical Inventory to the Early Music in the Newberry Library*. Boston: G.K.Hall, 1977. (Cited as Krummel)

Lasocki, David. "Professional recorder playing in England 1500-1740. II: 1640-1740." *Early Music* 20,2 (April 1982): 183-191.

Lesure, François. *Bibliographie des Éditions Musicales Publiées par Estienne Roger et Michel-Charles Le Cène*. Publications de la Société française de musicologie, series 2, vol.12. Paris: Heugel et Cie., 1969. (Cited as Roger)

Lesure, François, ed. *Catalogue de la Musique Impremée Avant 1800, Conservée dans les Bibliothèques Publiques de Paris*. Paris: Bibliothèque Nationale, 1981. (Cited as Lesure)

Lesure, François, ed. *Recueils imprimés XVIIIe siècle*. Répertoire International des Sources Musicales. Série BII. Munich: G.Henle Verlag, 1964. (Cited as RISM B II)

Library of Congress. Catalog Publication Division. *Music, Books on Music and Sound Recordings*. Washington: Library of Congress, 1953- . (Cited as NUC NBMSR)

Mainwaring, John. *Memoirs of the Life of the Late George Frederic Handel*. London: R. & J. Dodsley, 1760.

Marx, Hans Joachim. "Francesco Maria Ruspoli." In *The New Grove Dictionary of Music and Musicians* 16: 334. London: Macmillan, 1980.

Mayr, Giovanni Simone. *Biografie di Scrittori e Artisti Musicali Bergamaschi Nativi od Oriundi*. Bergamo: Pagnoncelli, 1875.

Medforth, Martin. "The Valentines of Leicester." *Musical Times* 122 (December 1981): 812-18.

Meyer, André. *Collection Musicale André Meyer*. 2 vols. Abbeville: F.Paillart, [1961]. (Cited as Meyer)

Minardi, Gian Paolo. "Parma." In *The New Grove Dictionary of Music and Musicians* 14: 235-237. London: Macmillan, 1980.

Newman, William S. *The Sonata in the Baroque Era*. Chapel Hill: University of North Carolina, 1959.

North, Roger. *Roger North on Music, Being a Selection from His Essays Written during the Years c.1695-1728*. Edited by John Wilson. London: Novello, [1959.]

xxi

Pogue, Samuel F. "Estienne Roger." In *The New Grove Dictionary of Music and Musicians* 16: 99-101. London: Macmillan, 1980.

Poole, H. Edmund and Donald W. Krummel. "Printing and publishing of music. II: Publishing." In *The New Grove Dictionary of Music and Musicians* 15: 260-274. London: Macmillan, 1980.

Raynor, Henry. *A Social History of Music from the Middle Ages to Beethoven.* New York: Taplinger, 1978.

Ringer, Alexander. "Education in music. IV,3: 1600-1800, Education of amateurs." In *The New Grove Dictionary of Music and Musicians* 6: 16-17. London: Macmillan, 1980.

Sadie, Stanley. "British chamber music, 1720-1790." Ph.D. dissertation, Cambridge University, 1958.

Sadie, Stanley. "Concert life in eighteenth-century England." *Proceedings of the Royal Musical Association* 85 (1958-1959): 17-30.

Sartori, Claudio. *Assisi, La Cappella della Basilica di S.Francesco. I. Catalogo del Fondo Musicale nella Biblioteca Comunale di Assisi.* Milan: Istituto Editoriale Italiano, 1962. (Cited as Sartori)

Sartori, Claudio. *Dizionario degli Editori Musicali Italiani.* Bibliotèca di bibliografia italiana, 32. Florence: Leo S. Olschki, 1958.

Schlager, Karlheinz, ed. *Einzeldrucke vor 1800.* Répertoire international des sources musicales. Série A I. Kassel: Barenreiter, 1971-1983. (Cited as RISM AI)

Schnapper, Edith B., ed. *British Union Catalogue of Early Music Printed Before the Year 1801.* 2 vols. London: Butterworths Scientific Publications, 1957. (Cited as BUCEM)

Smith, William C. *A Bibliography of Musical Works Published by John Walsh During the Years 1695-1720.* London: Printed for the Bibliographical society at the University Press, Oxford, 1948. (Cited as Walsh I)

Smith, William C. and Charles Humphries. *A Bibliography of the Musical Works Published by the Firm of John Walsh During the Years 1721-1766.* London: Bibliographical Society, 1968. (Cited as Walsh II)

Squire, W. Barclay. *Catalogue of Printed Music Published Between 1487-1800 Now in the British Museum.* 2 vols. London: Printed by the order of the Trustees, 1912. (Cited as BMCPM)

Thompson, James. *The History of Leicester in the Eighteenth Century.* History of Leicester, vol.2. Leicester: Crossley & Clark, 1871.

Tilmouth, Michael. "A calendar of references to music in newspapers published in London and the provinces, 1660-1719." *RMA Research Chronicle* 1 (1961).

_____. "Chamber music in England 1675-1720." Ph.D. dissertation, Cambridge University, 1959.

_____. "Chamber music, 2: Baroque." In *The New Grove Dictionary of Music and Musicians* 4: 114-115. London: Macmillan, 1980.

_____. "Nicola Matteis." *Musical Quarterly* 46,1 (January 1960): 22-40.

_____. "Robert Valentine." In *The New Grove Dictionary of Music and Musicians* 19: 494-495. London: Macmillan, 1980.

"Robert Valentine." In *Enciclopedia della Musica* 4: 457. Milan: Ricordi, 1964.

"Robert Valentine." In *Grosses vollständiges Universal-Lexikon aller Wissenschaften und Künste...*, vol.46. Halle: J.H. Zedler, 1732-1750.

"Robert Valentini." In *The Cyclopaedia, or, Universal Dictionary of Arts, Sciences, and Literature*, by Abraham Rees. Vol. 38. Philadelphia: Bradford, Murray, Fairman, 1819.

"Roberto Valentini." In *Encyclopèdie de la Musique*, vol. 3, 835. Paris: Fasquelle, 1961.

Venn, John, comp. *Alumni Cantabrigiensis.* Cambridge, England: University Press, 1922-54.

Vogel, Emil. *Die handschriften nebst den älteren Druckwerken der Musikabteilung der Herzogl. Bibliothek zu Wolfenbuttel.* Wolfenbuttel: J. Zwissler, 1890. (Cited as Vogel)

Walther, Johann Gottfried. *Musikalisches Lexikon.* Leipzig: Wolfgang Deer, 1732.

Willetts, Pamela J. *Handlist of Music Manuscripts Acquired 1908-1967.* London: British Museum, 1970. (Cited as Willetts)

Wollitz, Kenneth. *The Recorder Book.* New York: Knopf, 1982.

Wood, David A. *Music in the Harvard Libraries: A Catalogue of Early Printed Music and Books on Music in the Houghton Library and Eda Kuhn Loeb Music Library.* Cambridge: Harvard University Press, 1980. (Cited as Wood)

Woodfill, Walter L. *Musicians in English Society from Elizabeth to Charles I.* Princeton: Princeton University Press, 1953.

Wotquenne, Alfred. *Catalogue de la Bibliothèque du Conservatoire Royal de Musique de Bruxelles.* 4 vols. Brussels: J.J. Coosemans, 1898. Reprint. Brussels: Editions Culture et Civilisation, 1980. (Cited as Wotquenne)

Yorke-Long, Alan. *Music at Court; Four Eighteenth Century Studies.* London: Weidenfeld and Nicolson, [1954.]

Young, Percy M. *A History of British Music.* New York: W.W. Norton, 1967.

_____. "Robert Valentine." In *Die Musik in Geschichte und Gegenwart* 13: 1226-1227. Kassel: Barenreiter, 1966.

REFERENCE WORKS CITED IN SHORT FORM

BMCPM   W. Barclay Squire. *Catalogue of Printed Music Published between 1487-1800 Now in the British Museum.*

Bodemann   Eduard Bodemann, ed. *Die Handschriften der Königlichen Öffentlichen Bibliothek zu Hannover.*

BUCEM   Edith B. Schnapper, ed. *British Union Catalogue of Early Music Printed Before the Year 1801.*

Écorcheville   J. Écorcheville. *Catalogue du Fonds de Musique Ancienne de la Bibliothèque Nationale.*

Eitner   Robert Eitner. *Biographisch-Bibliographisches Quellen-Lexikon der Musiker und Musikgelehrten.*

Gasperini (Naples)   Associazione dei Musicologi Italiani. *Catalogo Generale... Città di Napoli.*

Gasperini (Parma)   Associazione dei Musicologi Italiani. *Catalogo Generale... Città di Parma.*

Giedde   Inge Bittman, comp. *Catalogue of Giedde's Music Collection...Royal Library of Copenhagen.*

Krummel   D.W.Krummel, ed. *Bibliographical Inventory to the Early Music in the Newberry Library.*

Lesure   François Lesure, ed. *Catalogue de la Musique Impremée Avant 1800, Conservée dans les Bibliothèques Publiques de Paris.*

Meyer   André Meyer. *Collection Musical André Meyer.*

NUC NBMSR   Library of Congress. *Music, Books on Music and Sound Recordings.*

RISM AI   Karlheinz Schlager, ed. *Einzeldrucke vor 1800.*

RISM BII   François Lesure. *Recueils Imprimés XVIIIe Siècle.*

Roger   François Lesure. *Bibliographie de Éditions Musicales Publieés par Estienne Roger et Michel-Charles Le Cène.*

Sartori Claudio Sartori. *Catalogo del Fondo Musicale nella Biblioteca Comunale di Assisi.*

Vogel Emil Vogel. *Die Handschriften...der Herzogl. Bibliothek zu Wolfenbuttel.*

Walsh I William C. Smith. *A Bibliography of Musical Works Published by John Walsh, 1695-1720.*

Walsh II William C. Smith and Charles Humphries. *A Bibliography of the Musical Works Published by the Firm of John Walsh, 1721-1766.*

Willetts Pamela J. Willetts. *Handlist of Music Manuscripts Acquired 1908-1967.* (British Museum)

Wood David A. Wood. *Music in the Harvard Libraries.*

Wotquenne Alfred Wotquenne. *Catalogue de la Bibliothèque du Conservatoire Royal de Musique de Bruxelles.*

LIBRARY SIGLA

B Bc   Conservatoire Royal de Musique, Bibliothèque, Brussels, Belgium

C Tu   University of Toronto, Faculty of Music (formerly, Royal Conservatory of Music) Library, Toronto, Ontario, Canada

D Hs   Staats- und Universitätsbibliothek, Musikabteilung, Hamburg, Germany

D MÜs   Santini-Bibliothek/Bibliothek des Bischoflichen Priesterseminars, Münster, Germany

D ROu   Universitätsbibliothek, Rostock, Germany

DK Kk   Det kongelige Bibliotek, Copenhagen, Denmark

F AG   Archives départementales, Agen, France

F Pc   Bibliothèque du Conservatoire national de musique, Paris, France (now at Bibliothèque nationale)

F Pn   Bibliothèque nationale, Paris, France

GB Cfm   Fitzwilliam Museum, Cambridge, Great Britain

GB Ckc   Rowe Music Library, King's College, Cambridge, Great Britain

GB Cu   University Library, Cambridge, Great Britain

GB CDp   Public Libraries, Central Library, Cardiff, Great Britain

GB DRc   Cathedral Library, Durham, Great Britain

GB Gm   Mitchell Library, Glasgow, Great Britain

GB Lcm   Royal College of Music, London, Great Britain

GB Lbl   British Library (formerly, British Museum), London, Great Britain

GB Olc   Lincoln College Library, Oxford, Great Britain

I Ac   Biblioteca comunale, Assisi, Italy

I BGi	Instituto musicale "Donizetti," Bergamo, Italy
I Fn	Biblioteca Nazionale Centrale, Florence, Italy
I PAc	Sezione Musicale della Biblioteca Palatina, now at Conservatorio "Arrigo Boito," Parma, Italy
I Rsc	Biblioteca Musicale Santa Cecilia (Conservatorio), Rome, Italy
S Skma	Kungliga Musikaliska Akademiens Bibliothek, Stockholm, Sweden
US Cn	Newberry Library, Chicago, Illinois, United States
US CHu	University of Virginia, Charlestown, Virginia, United States
US CA	Harvard University Music Libraries, Cambridge, Massachusetts, United States
US PHu	University of Pennsylvania, Music Library, Philadelphia, Pennsylvania, United States
US Su	University of Washington, Music Library, Seattle, Washington, United States
US Wc	Library of Congress, Music Division, Washington, D.C.

ORIGINAL WORKS

1 SONATAS OF THREE PARTS

for two violins & a bass with a through bass for ye organ
Opus 1, London, 1712
12 trio-sonatas for violins with continuo
(a D F C G d A Bb g Eb c E)

EARLY EDITIONS

JOHN WALSH / JOHN HARE, London, [1712]
4 parts, folio, engraved, violino primo 17 p., violino secundo 16 p., violoncello 16 p., organo 16 p.

| XII SONATAS | of three parts | for two | Violins & a Bass | with a | through Bass for ye Organ | Harpsicord or archLute | Compos'd by | Mr. Valentine at Rome. | Opera Prima. | London, | Printed for J. Walsh Servt. to her Maj^{ty} at ye Harp & Hoboy in Katherine | Street in ye Strand, & J. Hare at ye Viol & Flute in Cornhill near ye Royal Exchange. |

EXEMPLAR: British Library h.11.c (1).
DATING: Walsh I #419.
OTHER EXTANT COPIES: GB Lbl (another copy (h.II))--US CHu, Wc
CITATIONS: RISM AI V49; BUCEM II,1032; BMCPM II,614; Walsh I #419; Eitner X,25;
Walsh II #1480 (a later issue not extant).

MANUSCRIPTS

Paris. André Meyer Collection (Private).
Sonate a tre, doi violini col basso per l'organo...opera prima.
3 ms. parts, folio, violino primo 16 p., violino secundo 16 p., organo 16 p.

CITATIONS: Meyer,67.
NOTE: Unavailable for examination.

2   SONATE DI FLAUTO

a solo col basso per il cimbalo ò violone
Opus 2, Rome, 1708
12 sonatas for recorder with continuo
(F d G g d C e C a C Bb F)

EARLY EDITIONS

VITALE MASCARDI / FRANCESCO CAIFABRI, Rome 1708
Score, oblong folio, letterpress, 33 p.

| SONATE | DI | FLAVTO A SOLO. | Col Basso per il Cimbalo, ò violone | DEDICATE
ALL'ILLVSTRISSIMO SIG^R. CAVALIERE | IL SIGNOR THOMAS SAMVVELL | DA ROBERTO
VALENTINE INGLESE. | OPERA SECOND. | [printer's flower, 40 x 50 mm.] | [rule] | IN ROMA,
per il Mascardi 1708. Con licenza de'Superiori | [rule] | Si vendono da Francesco Caifabri all'Insegna
della Croce di Genoua'in Parione. |

DEDICATION

| ILLVSTRISSIMO SIGNORE | Signore, e Padron mio Colendis^{mo}. | [Ornamental initial in frame, 20
x 20 mm.] PERSVADENDOMI, ch'il desio da me sempre nudrito di | meritare presso V.S.
Illustriss^{ma}. possa esser stato principio, | di merito, me rendo ardito di pregare la di lei gran gentilez- |
za, perche si contenti, che glie lo palesi con l'osserta di queste Sona- | te, aborto del mio ingegno,
quali comparendo alla luce nobilitate | con il titolo del di lei pregiatissimo Nome, si ripromettono
sicuro l'ag- | gradimento de Virtuosi Professori, e saranno stimate meno mancanti di | quello, che lo
sono. Non isdegnipertanto V.S. Illustriss^{ma}. quest'attestato | della mia osseruanza, mentre facendole
humilissima riurenza, resto sem- | pre piu' ambizioso di farmi conoscere. | Di V.S. Illustriss^{ma}. |
Humiliss^{mo}., & Obligatiss^{mo}. Seruitore | Roberto Valentine. |

EXEMPLAR: British Library h.11.h.
OTHER EXTANT COPIES: F Pn--I PAc, Rsc.
CITATIONS: RISM AI V50; BUCEM II,1032; Gasperini (Parma),259; Écorcheville v.8 #156;
Lesure,618.

ESTIENNE ROGER, Amsterdam, [1709-1712]
Score, oblong folio, engraved, 35 p. Publisher's no. 41.

| Sonate | Di | Flauto a Solo | Col Basso per il Cimbalo o Violone | Dedicate All'illustrissimo Sig^{re}.
Cavaliere | il Signor Thomas Samwel | Da Roberto Valentine Inglese | Opera Seconda. | A
Amsterdam | Aux depens d'Estienne Roger Marchand Libraire. | Qui vend la Musique du monde la
plus correcte & qui s'engage de | la donner à meilleur marché que qui que ce sont quand | même il
deuroit la donner pour rien. |

EXEMPLAR: Universitätsbibliothek zu Rostock Mus. saec. XVIII 61[1].
DATING: Roger,83.
NOTICES: <u>Roger 1712</u> "Roberto Valentine opera seconda, XII sonates a une flute & Basse continue f 2.10" (Roger, 50); <u>Roger 1716</u> "41 Roberto Valentine opera seconda, XII sonates a une flute et b.c. f 2.10" (Roger, 83); <u>LeCene 1737</u> "41 Roberto Valentine opera seconda XII. Sonate a une Flute & Basse continue f 2.10" (Roger [Le Cène],25).
CITATIONS: RISM AI V51; Roger,83.
FACSIMILE: Montreal: Éditions les Gouts-Reunis, 1983.

PIERRE MORTIER, Amsterdam, [1709-1710]
Score, folio, engraved, 35 p.

| Sonate | Di | Flauto a Solo | Col Basso per il Cimbalo o Violone | Dedicate All'illustrissimo Sig[r]. Cavaliere | il Signor Thomas Samwell | Da Roberto Valentine Inglese | Opera Seconda | [printer's device 20 mm x 20 mm] | A Amsterdam | Chez Pierre Mortier sur le Vygendam. |

EXEMPLAR: Library of Congress M242.V16 op. 2.
OTHER EXTANT COPY: DK Kk.
CITATIONS: RISM AI V52; Giedde,123; NUC MBMSR 1953-57,883.

JOHN WALSH / JOHN HARE, London, [1713]
Score, folio, engraved, 34 p.

| [frame] | XII | Sonatas | or | Solos | for a | Flute | with a | Through-bass | for the | Harpsicord or Bass Violin | Compos'd by | M[r]: Valentine. at Rome | Opera [ms. II] | [rule] | London, Printed for J. Walsh at the Harp & Hoboy in | Katherine Street & J. Hare at the Viol & Flute in Cornhill. |

EXEMPLAR: British Library g.422 (1).
DATING: Walsh I #443.
OTHER EXTANT COPIES: B Bc--I BGi--US Cn, Wc.
CITATIONS: RISM AI V53; BUCEM II,1032; BMCPM II,614; Walsh I #443; NUC MBMSR 1953-57,883; Krummel,427; Eitner X,25.

JOHN WALSH / JOHN HARE, London, [1730]
Score, folio, engraved, 34 p. Publisher's no. 120.

| [frame] | Solos | for a | Flute | With a | Thorough Bass | for the | Harpsicord | or | Bass Violin | Compos'd by | M[r]. Valentine | at Rome | Opera 2[da] | [rule] | London Printed for I: Walsh Servant in Ordinary to his Majesty at the Harp & | Hoboy in Catherine Street in the Strand & I: Hare at the Viol & Flute in Cornhill | near ye Royal Exchange ["N[o.] 120." in ms.] |

EXEMPLAR: British Library h.11.a (I).
DATING: Walsh II #1481.
NOTICES: *Post Man* Nov. 29-Dec. 1, 1715 "Valentines 1st Book of Solos for a Flute and a Bass." (Walsh I #474)
CITATIONS: BUCEM II,1023; BMCPM II,614; Walsh I #443; Walsh II #1481; Lesure,618.
NOTE: Ms. publisher's number incorporates this edition into Walsh's numerical series of a later date, ca. 1730.

MANUSCRIPT

[Nos. 1, 7 & 11]

Hannover. Provinzialbibliothek. Handschr. IV 419[1].
Sonates pour la fleutte seul avec la basse.
Ms. score, folio (35 x 28 cm.), 11 leaves.

CITATION: Bodemann,72.
NOTE: No. 7 includes an added Allegro from no. 6.

MODERN EDITIONS

[Nos. 1, 7 & 11]

Drei Sonates fur Block- oder Querflöte und Cembalo eines unbekannten Meisters vom Ende des 17. Jahrhunderts; hrsg. von Albert Rodemann.--Hannover: A. Nagel, 1936 (Nagels Musik-Archiv, Nr. 121).

NOTE: Edited from the Hannover ms.; includes added Allegro in no. 7.

Three sonatas for flute and basso continuo.--Melville, N.Y.: Belwin Mills, 197-.

NOTE: Reprint of Nagels ed.

[Nos. 2, 5 & 12]

Drei Sonaten fur Block- oder Querflote und Basso continuo; hrsg. von Albert Rodemann.--Kassel: Nagels Verlag, c1940. (Nagels Musik-Archiv, Nr. 149).

[No. 9; arr.]

Sonata in A minor for viola; edited by Freda Dinn.--London: Schott, c1977 (Schott viola repertory, No. 5).--Edition 11263.

[No. 12; arr.]

Sonate en fa majeur pour trompette & piano ou orgue; reconstitution & realization de Jean Thilde.--Paris: G. Billaudot, c1970 (Collection Maurice Andre).

SOUND RECORDINGS

[No. 10; Arr.]

Art of the trumpet.--New York: VOX Cum Laude, p1982.--D-VCL 9015.
New York Trumpet Ensemble.

[Selections; arr.]

Trompette et orgue.--Paris: Harmonia Mundi, 197-.--HMU 901.

Francis Hardy, trumpet; Francis Chapelet, organ.

NOTE: "Reconstitution de Jean Thilde" includes no. 3, 1st mvt.; no. 2, 2nd mvt.; no. 5, 2nd and 3rd mvt.

3   SONATE DI FLAUTO

a solo col basso per il cimbalo o violone
Opus 3, Rome, 1710
12 sonatas for recorder with continuo
(d G F C a d G C a d g F)

NOTE: Sonatas 1,3,8 & 9 can be found arranged as trios (see 7. *Six Sonatas*, nos.
1-4) and as duos (see 26. *Six Sonatas of Two Parts*, nos. 1-4).

EARLY EDITIONS

VITALE MASCARDI, Rome, 1710
Score, oblong folio, letterpress, 49 p.

I SONATE DI FLAUTO A SOLO I <u>Col basso per il cimbalo o Violone</u> I <u>Dedicate all'Ills^{mo}</u>. Sig^{re}. <u>il</u>
Sig^{re}. <u>Giouanni</u> [engraved crest, 80 x 120 mm., title cut in surrounding banner] <u>Fleetwood Console</u>
<u>Britanico in Napoli</u> I <u>Da Roberto Valentine Inglese opera terza</u> [title page engraving signed in lower
right: Arnold v.westerhout] [colophon lower centre p. 49: IN ROMA, per il Mascardi, MDCCX. I
<u>Con licenza de'Superiori</u>.]

DEDICATION
I ILLVSTRISSIMO SIGNORE I [Ornamental initial in frame, 20 x 20 mm.] CONSAGRO a V.S.
Illustrissima in questa qualsiasi Composizione il terzo I parto del mio debole ingegno, ed ho ferma
sede, che bastera l'alto suo I Nome per disenderlo dalle maledicenze de'Zoili, e dagl'l[sic]nsulti di Co-
I biasimare [swash E] I le altrui. La cognizione, che ho della benignita del suo gran cuore mi I
lusinga la speranza, che sia per receuerlo in argomento del mio riuerente ossequio, ed I il sapere, che
fra le virtudi, che adornano la sua non puo meritare applausi dalla pouerta del mio stile; mi sa
credere, I che vorra Ella rendere glorioso il mio ardire, e <u>Vonilissimo</u>, <u>Deuotissimo</u>, & <u>Obligatissimo</u>
<u>Seruitore</u> I Roberto Valentine. I

EXEMPLAR: British Library e.22.e
CITATION: RISM AI V56.

ESTIENNE ROGER, Amsterdam, [1709-1712]
Score, oblong folio, engraved, 26 p. Publisher's no. 121.

I XII Sonate I A Flauto Solo col Basso Continuo I Di I Roberto Valentine Inglese I Opera Terza. I A
Amsterdam I Chez Estienne Roger Marchand Libraire. I N°. 121. I

EXEMPLAR: British Library e.22
DATING: Roger,83.

12

OTHER EXTANT COPIES: **GB** Ckc--**US** Wc.
NOTICES: <u>Roger 1716</u> "121 Roberto Valentine opera terza, XII Sonates à une flûte et bc. f.
        2.10" (Roger,83); <u>LeCene 1737</u> "121 Roberto Valentine poera Terza XII Sonate à
        une Flûte & Basse contin. f 2.10." (Roger [Le Cène],25).
CITATIONS: RISM AI V54; Roger,83; BUCEM II, 1032; BMCPM II, 614; NUC MBMSR
        1953-57,883 [LCCN 45-30922].

JOHN WALSH / JOHN HARE, London, [1721]
Score, folio, engraved, 37 p.

| [frame] | XII | Sonatas | or | Solos | for a | Flute | with a Through-bass | for the | Harpsicord or Bass
Violin | Compos'd by | M^r: Valentine. at Rome | Opera Terza | [rule] | London, Printed for J. Walsh
at the Harp & Hoboy in | Katherine Street & J. Hare at the Viol & Flute in Cornhill. |

EXEMPLAR: British Library h.II.a (2).
DATING: Walsh I #458.
OTHER EXTANT COPIES: **B** Bc (2 copies)--**C** Tu--**GB** Ckc, Lbl (another copy   i.26 (4))--**S**
        Skma.
NOTICES: <u>Walsh 1721</u> "Valentines 3rd Solos, for a Flute & a Bass." (Walsh I #458)
CITATIONS: RISM AI V55; BUCEM II,1032; BMCPM II,614; Walsh I #458 (c.f.475);
        Eitner X,25.

MANUSCRIPT

[Nos. 1-11]

Wolfenbüttel. Herzog-August-Bibliothek. Codex Guelph 298, f. 55-72.
Solo flavto 1712 [from cover]
Ms. parts, quarto (16 x 19.5 cm.), 17 leaves, foliated 55-72, bound.

CITATION: Vogel,63.
NOTES: flute part only.

MODERN EDITIONS

[No. 5]

Sonate [A moll] von Robert Valentine...Bearbeitung von A. Moffat--Berlin: N. Simrock, 1899.--Pl.
No.: 11230. (Meister-Schule der alten Zeit: Sammlung klassischer Violin-Sonaten; 17)

NOTES: 3rd mvt. replaced by his op.6, no.2, 2nd mvt.

Compositionen und Arrangements; 12 Violinstucke klassischer Meister von Alfred Moffat Opus 43,
Nr. 4--Berlin: N. Simrock, c1899--Pl. no. 11141--Caption title: Sarabanda / Valentine.

NOTE: 3rd mvt. only.

4   BALLETTI DA CAMERA A TRE

cioè due violini con il basso
Opus 4, Rome, 1711
12 trio-sonatas for violins with continuo
(b e C A F a D g d E♭ B♭ f#)

EARLY EDITION

VITALE MASCARDI, Rome, 1711
3 parts, quarto, letterpress, violino primo 36 p., violino secondo 36 p., basso 36 p.

| Violino Primo | [rule] | BALLETTI | DA | CAMERA | A trè, cioè Violini con il Basso | DEDICATI | ALL'ILLVSTRISSIMO SIGNORE | CRISTOFANO | BERNARDO | BARON DI KATTEN | DA ROBERTO VALENTINE. | Opera Quarta. | [three printer's flowers] | [rule] | In Roma per il Mascardi MDCCXI. con licenza d'Superiori. |

DEDICATION

| Ill^MO. Sig^RE,. Sig., e Pad^ON. Col^MO. | [large space on page, the remainder of the text on this page is at the very bottom] | ESCE [ornamental initial in frame] questo mio debol parto alla | luce composto di Sonate, che mi | lufingo, che siano per riuscire molto grate al no- | bil orecchio di V.S. | Illustrifs., e tanto maggior- | [Page 2] | mente verranno dal Mondo applaudite, in | quanto sarrano fregiate col chiaro nome di V.S. | Illustrissima, che le servirà di forte scudo contro | la potenza degli inimici della virtù; Essendo | ben noto all'universo quanto sia il dilei no- | bil animo proclive in favorire i virtuosi, che | ne acquista da per tutto il celebre grido di | Mecenate. Si Compiaccia adunque V.S. Illu- | strisima gradire questo picciol tributo, che le pre- | sento, che servirà per un attestato della mia | Devotione, con cui me le ratifico fin alle ceneri. | Di V.S. Illustrissima | Humiliss., & Obligatiss. Servitore | Roberto Valentine. |

EXEMPLAR: British Library e.22.a.
CITATIONS: RISM AI V57; BUCEM II,1032.

I. Preludio-Adagio   II. Allemande-Allegro

1

III. Sarabande-Adagio   IV. Giga-Allegro

I. Preludio-Adagio   II. Allemande-Allegro

III. Sarabanda-Adagio   IV. Gavotta-Allegro

I. Preludio (Adagio)   II. Corrente-Allegro

III. Sarabanda-Adagio   IV. Giga (Allegro)

I. Preludio-Adag(io)   II. Allemanda-Allegro

III. Sarabanda-Adagio   IV. Giga-Allegro

I. Preludio-Adagio   II. Allemanda-Allegro

11

III. Sarabanda-Adagio   IV. Presto

I. Preludio-Adagio   II. Allemanda-Allegro

12

III. Adagio   IV. Giga-Allegro

5   SIX SONATAS

for two violins, two hoboy's
or German flutes with a thorough bass for the
harpsicord or bass violin
Opus 4, London, 1715
6 trio-sonatas for violins, oboes, or flutes with continuo
(A Bb D E A Bb)

NOTE: For duo arrangement see 25. *Six Sonatas of Two Parts.*

EARLY EDITION

DANIEL WRIGHT, London, [1715]
3 parts, folio, engraved, violino primo 12 p., violino secondo 12 p., basso 12 p.

|[Lettering in cartouche within an ornamental frame] | Six | SONATAS for Two | Violins two Hoboy's | or German Flutes w^th| A Thorough BASS for | The HARPSICORD | or Bass Violin Composd | By Mr Valentini lieving | In Rome | Opera Quarta | Note all the other Works | of this author may be had | Where this is sold | London. Printed for the Author at the Old Post Office in [Rusel] Street [Covent Garden] | Daniel Wright Musical Instrument Maker, next to the Sun-Tavern in Holborn. |

EXEMPLAR: British Library h.11.f.
DATING: BUCEM II,1032.
OTHER EXTANT COPY: **D Hs** (1st violin only).
CITATIONS: RISM AI V58; BUCEM II,1032; BMCPM II,614.
NOTE: Imprint illegible in exemplar.

6 SONATA A FLAUTO SOLO COL BASSO

Opus 5, Rome, 171-
12 sonatas for recorder with continuo
(C a F C Bb e G F F F C F)

EARLY EDITIONS

[Nos. 1-6]

FRANCESCHINI, Rome.
Score, oblong folio, engraved, 21 p.

| [cartouche] | SONATA A FLAVTO SOLO COL BASSO | Dedicata | All' Illus^{mo} Sig^{re} il Sig^r Cavalier Tomasso | Coke | Da Roberto Valentine Inglese opera quinta parte prima | Dom. Franceschini ferit Roma Sup. perm |

DEDICATION
| [frame] | Illustrissimo Sig.^{re} | Il genio singolare, che nutrisce V.S. Ill:^{ma} uerso le Virtù fà che risieda nel animo. | vgual affetto col patrocinio dè Virtuosi. Onde persuaso anch'io (che frà quelli | l'infimo grado m'ascriuo) di questa benigna propensione d'V.S. Ill:^{ma} sono à con= | sacrarle questa prima parte dell'Opera quinta di sonate di Flauto. Il tri= | buto è debole à riflesso del merito ben grande d'V.S. Ill:^{ma}, mà spero, che sarà | grandito dalla sua grandezza in puro segno del mio humilissimo ossequio, à | fine che l'opera sia sfolgorata coi suoi splendori, e resa gloriosa sotto la sua Pro= | tezzione. cosi la supplico con tutto il seruore della mia deuotissima osseruan= | di V.S. Illustrissima | [lower right hand corner] Den^{mo}, et Oblig.^{mo} Seruitore | Roberto Valentine |

> EXEMPLAR: Library of Congress M242.v16 op.5.
> CITATION: RISM AI V65.

JEANNE ROGER, Amsterdam.
Score, folio, engraved, 22 p. Publisher's no. 453.

| VI Sonate | à Flauto Solo e Basso Continuo | DI | Roberto Valentine | Inglese | Opera Sesta [!] | A Amsterdam | Chez Jeanne Roger | N° 453 |

> EXEMPLAR: Library of Congress ML30.4c no. 1432 Miller.
> CITATION: RISM AI V64.
> NOTE: no. 5 transposed.

JOHN WALSH / JOHN HARE, London, [1718]
Score, folio, engraved, 36 p. Publisher's no. 122.

| [frame] | XII | SONATAS | or | SOLOS | for a | FLUTE | with a | THROUGH BASS | for the | HARPSICORD | or | BASS VIOLIN | Compos'd by | M^r: Valentine at Rome | Opera Quinta | [rule] | London Printed for I: Walsh Servt. in Ordinary to his Majesty at ye Harp & Hoboy in Catherine | [Street indecipherable on film] in ye Strand: & I: Hare at ye Viol & Flute in Cornhill near ye Royall Exchange |

> EXEMPLAR: British Library h.11.a.(3).
> DATING: Walsh II #1485.
> OTHER EXTANT COPIES: **C** Tu--**GB** Ckc--**US** Wc.
> NOTICES: *Post Boy*, Dec. 6-9, 1718. (Walsh I #554)
> CITATIONS: RISM AI V63; Walsh I #554; Walsh II #1485.

MODERN EDITION

[Nos. 1, 2 & 6]

Drei Sonaten für Altblockflöte, Querflöte, Violine und Basso continuo, hrsg. von Frank Nagel.--Wolfenbüttel: Möseler Verlag. c1975 (Hausmusik, 122).

7   SIX SONATAS

for 2 violins & a bass
Opus 6, London, 1715
6 trio-sonatas for 2 violins with continuo
(a D G g d B♭)

NOTE: For duo arrangement see 26. *Six Sonatas of Two Parts.*
Sonatas 1-4 are trio versions of 3. *Sonate di Flauto*, nos. 1,3,8 & 9.

EARLY EDITION

DANIEL WRIGHT / J. YOUNG, London, [1715]
3 parts, folio, engraved, violino primo 11 p., violino secondo 11 p., basso continuo 6 p.

| [frame] | SIX | SONATAS | for 2 Violins & a Bass | by | Mʳ. Valentine | at Rome. | Opera Sexta |
LONDON, | Printed & Sold by D. Wright, next yᵉ Sun Tavern, at yᵉ corner of | Brook-street in
Holborn. & J. Young at yᵉ Dolphin & Crown yᵉ West end | of Sᵗ. Pauls Church Yard, where all yᵉ
works of this Author. may be had. |

EXEMPLAR: British Library h.11.g.(1)
DATING: BUCEM II,1032.
CITATIONS: RISM AI V67; BUCEM II,1032; BMCPM II,614.

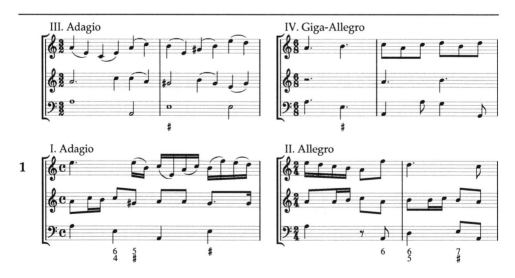

8   SIX SONATAS

of two parts for two flutes
Opus 7, London, 1720
6 sonatas for 2 recorders
(A D Bb A c a)

EARLY EDITIONS

DANIEL WRIGHT, London, [1720]
2 parts, folio, engraved, violino primo 6 p., violino secondo 6 p.

| [frame] | Six | SONATAS | of two Parts | for two | [ms. "FLUTES or"] | VIOLINS [label] |
Compos'd by | Mr Valentine | at Rome | Opera 7ma. | Note all ye Choisest Works of this author may
be had where these are sold | [rule] | London Printed and sold by Daniel Wright next the Sun Tavern
the Corner of Brook | Street in Holbourn. |

    EXEMPLAR: British Library h.11.g.(2).
    DATING: BUCEM II,1032.
    CITATIONS: RISM AI V73; BUCEM II,1032; BMCPM II,614; Wood #1520.

DANIEL WRIGHT, London, [1721]
2 parts, folio, engraved, violino primo 6 p., violino secondo 6 p.

| [frame] | Six | SONATAS | of two Parts | for two | FLUTES | Compos'd by | Mr Valentine | at Rome
| Opera 7ma. | Note all ye Choisest Works of this author may be had where these are sold | [rule] |
London Printed and sold by Daniel Wright next the Sun Tavern the Corner of Brook | Street in
Holbourn. |

    EXEMPLAR: British Library g. 297 (1).
    DATING: BUCEM II,1032.
    OTHER EXTANT COPIES: GB Ckc--US CA.
    CITATIONS: RISM AI V72; BUCEM II,1032; BMCPM II,615.
    NOTE: Cancel label reading "Violins" covers the word "Flutes" on title-page of the violino
              primo part in Harvard (US CA) copy. These three copies and the one listed above
              are probably all states of the same edition.

JOHN WALSH / JOHN HARE, London, [1730]
2 parts, folio, engraved, flauto primo 6 p., flauto secondo 6 p.

| Six | SONATAS | of two Parts | for two | FLUTES | Compos'd by | M^r: Valentine | at Rome | Opera
7ma. | [rule] | London Printed for I: Walsh Servt. in Ordinary to his Majesty at the Harp & Hoboy |

in Catherine Street in the Strand: and I: Hare at the Viol and Flute in Cornhill | near the Royall Exchange. |

EXEMPLAR: British Library h.11.j.
DATING: Walsh II #1487.
OTHER EXTANT COPY: US Wc (2nd flute only).
NOTICES: *Post Boy*, Jan 28-30, 1720. (Walsh I #575)
CITATIONS: RISM AI V71; BUCEM II p.1032; Walsh I #575; Walsh II #1487.

9 SIX SETTS OF AIRES AND A CHACOON

for two flutes & a bass
Opus 8, London, 1718
6 trio-sonatas and chaconne for 2 recorders with continuo
(C a G d e C F)

EARLY EDITION

JOHN WALSH / JOHN HARE, London, [1718]
3 parts, folio, engraved, flauto primo 8 p., flauto secondo 8 p., basso continuo 8 p.

| [frame] | Six Setts of | AIRES | and a | CHACOON | for two | FLUTES & a BASS | Compos'd by |
M^r: Valentine | at Rome | [rule] | Note there are several Curious Pieces as Solos and Sonatas for
Flutes Com | pos'd by this Author, which may be had where these are Sold. | [rule] | London Printed
for | Walsh Servt in Ordinary to his Majesty at the | Harp and Hautboy in Katherine street in the
Strand, and | Hare | at the Viol and Flute in Cornhill, near the Royal Exchange |

EXEMPLAR: British Library h.250.c (6).
DATING: BUCEM II,1032.
OTHER EXTANT COPIES: **GB** Cfm, CDp, DRc, Gm.
NOTICES: *Post Boy*, Nov. 18-20, 1718. (Walsh I #552)
CITATIONS: RISM AI V85; BUCEM II,1032; BMCPM II,614; Walsh I #552; Walsh II
#1475.

MODERN EDITIONS

[No. 1]

Trio sonata in C major, for two treble recorders and piano, or harpsichord, with violoncello, or
viola da gamba ad lib.; ed. W. Pearson.--London: Schott, c1940 (Edition Schott, 10011).

[No. 2]

Trio sonata in a minor for two treble recorders and piano, or harpsichord, with violoncello, or viola
da gamba ad lib.; ed. W. Pearson.--London: Schott, [196-?] (Edition Schott, 10084).

[No. 4]

Trio sonata in d minor, for two treble recorders and piano, or harpsichord, with violoncello, or viola
da gamba ad lib.; ed. by W. Pearson.--London: Schott, c1957. (Edition Schott, 10605).

[No. 7]

Chaconne für 2 Altblockflöten und Bc; ed. by Salkeld.--Vienna: Universal Edition, [196-?] (Universal Edition, 12632).

SOUND RECORDING

[No. 7]

<u>In</u>   Flauto dolce.--Bärenreiter-Musicaphon, [1981?].--1924.
Manfred Harras, Marianne Lüthi, recorders; Hannelore Müller, viola da gamba; Rudolf Scheidegger, cembalo.

NOTE: Transposed.

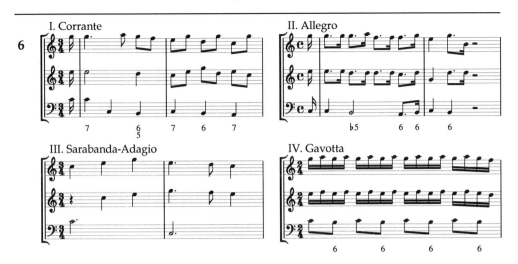

10   SEVEN SETTS OF AIRES

for 2 flutes & a bass
Opus 9, London, 1720
7 trio-sonatas for 2 recorders with continuo
(F C d F F g c)

EARLY EDITIONS

JOHN WALSH / JOHN HARE, London, [1720]
3 parts, folio, engraved, flauto primo 6 leaves, fluto [sic] secondo 6 leaves, basso 6 leaves.

| [frame] | Seven | Setts of Aires | for two | Flutes & a Bass | Consisting of | Preludes Allmands | Corants Sarabands | Marches Minuets | Gavotts and Jiggs | Being familliar & easey for Young | Practitioners in Concert | Compos'd by | Mr Robt. Valentine | at Rome Opera Nona | [rule] | London, Printed for & sold by I: Walsh Servt. to his Majesty at ye Harp & Hoboy in | Catherine Street in ye Strand: & I: Hare at the Viol & Flute in Cornhill near ye Royal Exchange. |

EXEMPLAR: British Library g. 297 (2).
DATING: BMCPM II,614.
OTHER EXTANT COPIES: **GB** Gm--**US** Wc (2nd flute only).
NOTICES: *Post Boy*, Oct. 14-17, 1721. (Walsh II #1476)
CITATIONS: RISM AI V76; BUCEM II,1032; BMCPM II,614; Walsh II #1476.

MODERN EDITIONS

[Nos. 1,2, & 3]

Trio-sonaten für zwei Altblockflöten in f', (Querflöten oder Violinen) und Cembalo (Klavier) Gambe/Violoncello ad lib; Hrsg. von Hildemarie Peter.--Berlin: R. Lienau (vormals Schlesinger) c1957.

[No. 7]

In   Triosonaten alter englischer Meister, für zwei Altblockflöten und Basso continuo; Hugo Ruf, comp.--Kassel: Bärenreiter. c1973. (Hortus musicus, 217).

7

11 SEVEN SETTS OF AIRES

for two flutes & a bass
Opus 10, London, 1720
7 trio-sonatas for 2 recorders with continuo
(F F F C F Bb d)

EARLY EDITIONS

DANIEL WRIGHT, London, [1720]
3 parts, folio, engraved, flauto primo 6 p., fluto [sic] secondo 6 p., basso 6 p.

| [frame] | Seven | Setts of Aires | for two | Flutes & a Bass | Consisting of | Preludes Allmands
Corant⁵ | Sarabands Marches Minuets | Gavots and Jiggs | Being familliar and easey for Young
Practitioners in Concert | Compos'd by | Mʳ. Robert Valentine | at Rome Opera 10ᵗʰ | [rule] |
Lon<d>on Printed and sold by Daniel Wright Musical instrument-maker and | musick Printer next
the Sunn Tavern the corner of Brook-Street in Holborn there | any Gentleman may be supply'd with
all sorts of Musick Books and Songs |

EXEMPLAR: British Library g. 297 (3).
DATING: BMCPM II,614.
OTHER EXTANT COPY: US Wc
CITATIONS: RISM AI V77; BUCEM II,1032; BMCPM II,614.

JOHN WALSH/JOHN HARE, London, [1720]
3 parts, folio, engraved.

| [frame] | Seven | Setts of Aires | for two | Flutes & a Bass | Consisting of | Preludes Allmands |
Corants Sarabands | Marches Minuets | Gavotts and Jiggs | Being familliar & easey for Young |
Practitioners in Concert | Compos'd by | Mʳ Robᵗ. Valentine | at Rome Opera ["Decima" in ms.] |
[rule] | London, Printed for & sold by I: Walsh Servᵗ. to his Majesty at yᵉ Harp & Hoboy in |
Catherine Street in yᵉ Strand: & I: Hare at the Viol & Flute in Cornhill near yᵉ Royal Exchange. |

EXEMPLAR: British Library h. 11. b.
DATING: BUCEM II,1032.
OTHER EXTANT COPIES: **GB** CKc, Gm (incomplete), Lbl--**US** Wc (2nd flute only).
NOTICE: *Post Boy*, Dec. 7-9, 1721. (Walsh II #1478)
CITATIONS: RISM AI V78; BUCEM II,1032; BMCPM II,614; Walsh II #1478.

III. Sarabanda-Adagio

IV. Minuet

7

I. Adagio

II. Allegro

III. Adagio

IV. Minuet

12   SONATAS OR SOLOS

for a flute with a thorough bass for the harpsicord or bass violin
Opus 11, London, 1727
6 sonatas for recorder with continuo
(F a B♭ a E♭ C)

EARLY EDITION

JOHN WALSH / JOSEPH HARE, London, [1727]
Score, folio, engraved, 22 p. Publisher's no. 123.

| [frame] | SONATAS | or | SOLOS | for a | FLUTE | With a | Thorough Bass | for the | HARPSICORD | or | Bass Violin | Compos'd by | M^r: Valentine | at Rome. Opera XIth. | [rule] | London. Printed for & sold by I: Walsh servant to his Majesty at ye Harp | and Hoboy in Catherine street in ye strand. and Ioseph Hare at the Viol and | Flute in Cornhill near the Royal Exchange | ["No. 123" in ms.]|

EXEMPLAR: British Library h.11.a.(4).
DATING: BUCEM II,1032.
OTHER EXTANT COPIES: **GB** Ckc (2 copies).
NOTICES: *London Journal*, Sept. 16, 1727. (Walsh II #1490)
CITATIONS: RISM AI V79; BUCEM II,1032; BMCPM II,614; Walsh II #1490-1.

MANUSCRIPT

Parma. Biblioteca palatina sezione musicale.
[12] Sonate a flauto solo con basso, opera XI, del sig.re Roberto Valentine Inglese.
Ms. score, oblong quarto, [42] leaves.

CITATIONS: Gasperini (Parma),259.
NOTE: Unavailable for examination.

MODERN EDITION

[No. 3]

In   Sonaten alter Englischer Meister, für Altblockflöte und Basso continuo; Hugo Ruf, comp.--Kassel: Bärenreiter, 1971. (Hortus musicus, 208-209).

SOUND RECORDING

[No. 3]

<u>In</u>   English recorder sonatas.--Musical Heritage Society, 1974.--MHS 1885.
     Ferdinand Conrad, recorder; Hugo Ruf, harpsichord; Gunhild Münch-Holland, viola da gamba.

13   12 SOLOS

for a violin with a thorough bass for the harpsicord or bass violin
Opus 12, London, 1728
12 sonatas for violin with continuo
(A c G F E♭ D g C b B♭ E B)

EARLY EDITION

JOHN WALSH / JOSEPH HARE, London, [1728]
Score, folio, engraved, 50 p.

| [frame] | XII | SOLOS | for a | VIOLIN | with a | THOROUGH BASS | for the | HARPSICORD | or | BASS VIOLIN | Compos'd by | M^r: Valentine at Rome | Opera XIIth. | [rule] | London. Printed for and sold by I: Walsh Servant to his Majesty at the Harp & Hoboy | in Catherine street in the Strand. and Ioseph Hare at the Viol and Flute in Cornhill | near the Royall Exchange. |

EXEMPLAR: British Library h.11.k.
DATING: Walsh II #1492
OTHER EXTANT COPIES: **D Hs--GB Cu.**
NOTICES: *Country Journal; or, The Craftsman*, March 30, 1728 (Lately published); *Daily Journal*, Jan. 29, 1730, (New Musick and Editions of Musick, Just published). (Walsh II #1492)
CITATIONS: RISM AI V82; BUCEM II,1032; Walsh II #1492.

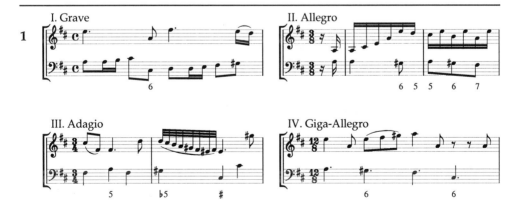

14   SONATE

per il flauto traversiero, col basso che possono service per violino,
mandola, et oboé
Opus 12, Rome, 1730
6 sonatas for flute, violin, mandola, or oboe with continuo
(A d G g e D)

EARLY EDITIONS

ANTONIO CLETON, Rome, 1730
Score, oblong folio, engraved, 26 p.

|[Frame; lettering inside cartouche; all capital Iˢ have dots over them] | SONATE | PER IL FLAVTO TRAVERSIERO, COL BASSO CHE POSSONO | SERVIRE PER VIOLINO MANDOLA, ET OBOÉ | DEDICATE ALL'ILLᵐᵒ: ET ECCᵐᵒ. Sʳᵉ. | D. GENNARO GIROLᵒ. VITALIANO MOCCIA | DVCA DELL'ORATINO, E ROCCA ASPROMONTE | BARONE DEL BVSTO, E MONTE VAIRANO &c | DA ROBERTO VALENTINI INGLESE | OPERA XII. | [printer's signature outside of cartouche, but within frame] | Incisa da Antonio Cleton Roma [large space] Con licenza de Superiori |

DEDICATION
| Illᵐᵒ et Eccᵐᵒ: Sigʳᵉ: | L'Amore singolare, che V.E. nodrisce uerso di ogni piú riguardeuole scienza, e l' | antica umile seruitú, che mi glorio di professarle mi hanno somministrato fiducia | di consecrarle questi miei componimenti; non giá che stimi poter questi appagare | la sublimitá del suo spirito, e la profonditá del suo intelletto; má perche deriuando essi | (tutto che parto d'un debole ingegno) da un principio nobilè, e uirtuoso, come é l'armonia de | concenti musicali, non posso fare á meno di credere, che sia per degnarli di un benigno | gradimento, et auualorarli colla sua efficacissima protezione, quale supplico anche all'Auto= | re uoler generosamente compartire, mentre pieno di uenerationе, e d'ossequio, mi dó l'onore di | dirny. Roma piño Maggio 1730 | D.V.E. | [in lower right hand corner] Vmo Serᵒ: Obligᵐᵒ | Roberto Valentiny |

EXEMPLAR: British Library e.22.d.
CITATIONS: RISM AI V80; BUCEM II,1032; BMCPM II,615.

MAUPETIT / BOIVIN / LE CLERC, Paris, [1741]
Score, folio, engraved, 26 p.

| [lettering inside cartouche] | SONATE | Per il Flauto traversiero, col Basso | Che possono servire | PER VIOLINO, MANDOLA, ET OBOÉ. | Dedicate | AL L'ILLUSTRISSᵐᵒ. ET ECCELLENTISᵐᵒ. SIGNʳᵉ. | D. GENNARO GIROLᵒ. | VITALIANO MOCCIA, | Duca del l'Oratino, e Rocca aspromonte | Barone del Busto, e Monte variano &c. | [ornamental rule] | DA ROBERTO VALENTINI, Inglese. | Opera XIIª. | [short rule] | Se VEND A Paris CHEZ | Mʳ Maupetit, Cloître Sʳ. germain l'auxerrow | M. Boivin m'.rue St. Honore a la régle d'or, et | M. Le Clerc m.'rue du roule, à

la Croix d'or. | Avec Privilége du Roi. | Prix 3ᴸᵗ. [design] en blanc. | [enclosed in small section at the bottom of the cartouche] La musique grarde par Mˡˡᵉ. Estien, | et Tornement par Marin. |

DEDICATION

| [frame] | Illᵐᵒ. et Ecclᵐᵒ. Sigʳᵉ | L'Amore singolare, che V.E. nodrisce verso di ogni piú ri- | guarde vole Scienza, e l'antica umile servitú, che mi glorio di | professarle mi hanno somministrato fiducia di consecrarle questi | mici componimenti; non giá che stimi poter questi appagare la su- | blimitá del suo Spirito, e la profonditá del suo intelletto; ma perche | derivando essi (tutto che parto d'un debole ingegno) dá un princi- | pio nobile e virtuoso, come é l'armonia de concenti musicali, non pos- | so fare á meno di credere, che sia per degnarli di un benigno gra- | dimento, et auvalorarli colla sua efficacissima protezione, quale | Supplico anche all'autore voler generosamente compartire, mentre | pieno di venerazione, e d'ossequio, mi dó l'onore di dirny. | D.V.E. | Viño Serʳᵉ. Obligᵐᵒ. | Roberto Valentini |

EXEMPLAR: Bibliothèque nationale Vm7. 6465.
DATING: Wotquenne, #5829.
OTHER EXTANT COPIES: B Bc--F Pc (Imprint: Estien, Boivin, LeClerc).
CITATIONS: RISM AI V81; Lesure,618; Wotquenne #5829; Écorchville v.9,156.

MODERN EDITION

Drei Sonaten für Querflöte (Violine, Oboe, c"--Sopran-, c'--Tenor Blockflöte) und Cembalo (Klavier) Gambe/Violoncello ad lib; Hrsg. von Hildemarie Peter.--Berlin-Lichterfelde: R. Lienau (vormals Schlesinger). c1957. (Zusammenspiel für Blockflöten).

15 SONATAS OR SOLOS

for a German flute with a thorough bass for the harpsicord or bass violin
Opus 13, London, 1735
6 sonatas for flute with continuo
(e g D F F d)

EARLY EDITION

JOHN WALSH, London, [1735]
Score, folio, engraved, 26 p. Publisher's no. 541.

| [frame] | SONATAS | or | SOLOS | For a German | FLUTE | with a Thorough Bass for the | HARPSICORD | or | BASS VIOLIN | Compos'd by | M^r: Valentine | at Rome. Opera XIIIth. | [rule] | The following Works of this Author may be had where these are Sold (Viz) 12 Sonatas | for 2 Violins & a Bass Opera 1ma. 12 Solos for a Flute & a Bass Opera 2do. 12 Solos | for a Flute & a Bass Opera 3ra. 6 Sonatas for 2 Flutes Opera 4ta. 12 Solos for a Flute & | a Bass Opera 4ta. 6 Sonatas for 2 Flutes Op: 6ta. 6 Sonatas for 2 Flutes Op: 7th. 6 Sonatas | for 2 Flutes & a Bass Op: 8th. Sonatas for 2 Flutes & a Bass Op: 9th. Sonatas for 2 Flutes | & a Bass Op: 10th. 6 Solos for a Flute & a Bass Op: 11th. 12 Solos for a Violin & a Bass Op: 12th. | [rule] | London. Printed for & Sold by Iohn Walsh Musick-Printer & Instrument-maker to his Majes- | ty at the Harp & Hoboy in Catherine Street in the Strand. | N°. 541 |

EXEMPLAR: British Library h.11.a. (5.).
DATING: BUCEM II,1032.
OTHER EXTANT COPIES: **B** Bc--**US** Cn, Wc.
NOTICES: *London Evening-Post*, April 26-29, 1735. (Walsh II #1494)
CITATIONS: RISM AI V83; BUCEM II,1032; BMCPM II,615; Walsh II #1494.

V. Minuet-Allegro

I. Adagio

II. Allegro

III. Adagio

IV. Giga-Allegro

I. Grave

II. Allegro

III. Adagio

IV. Giga-Allegro

I. Adagio

II. Allegro

III. Adagio

IV. Vivace

V. Giga-Allegro

16   LA VILLEGGIATURA

a violino solo col basso
Opus 13, Rome
6 sonatas for violin with continuo
(B♭ E F E♭ A D)

EARLY EDITION

ANTONIO CLETON, Rome.
Score, oblong folio, engraved, 20 p.

| [frame] | LA VILLEGGIATVRA | A VIOLINO SOLO COL BASSO | DEDICATA | ALL'ILLVSTRISSIMO SIG^re., IL SIG^r. CAVALIERE | GIORGIO PITT | DA ROBERTO VALENTINI INGLESE | OPERA XII | [ornamental frame] | [printer's signature below frame] | Si uendono dal Libraro al Corso sotto Verospi in Roma, [space] Antonius Cleton Scul: Sup: per: | et anco dall'Autore |

DEDICATION
| Illmo Sig^re. [ornamental script] | Il genio singolare, che nutrisce V.S. Illma uerso le Virtù fà, che risieda nell'= | animo ugual' affetto col patrocinio de Virtuosi; Onde persuaso anch'io (che | frà quelli l'infimo grado m'ascriuo) di questa benigna propenzione di V.S. Illma | sono à Consacrarle quest'Opera decima tersa di sonate a Violino solo col Basso. | Il tributo è debole a riflesso del merito ben grande di V.S. Illma, ma spero, che | sarà grandito dalla sua grandezza in puro segno del mio humilissimo ossequiò | a fine che l'opera sia sfolgorata coi suoi splendori, e resa gloriosa sotto la sua pro= | tezzione. Cosi la supplico con tutto il feruore della mia deuotissima osseruanza, | mentre resto con uantarmi per sempre. | D.V.S. Illma | Deu^mo, et Oblig^mo: Sèruitore | Roberto Valentine |

EXEMPLAR: Conservatoire Royal de Musique de Bruxelles. Fètis #5830.
CITATIONS: RISM AI V84; Wotquenne, #5830.

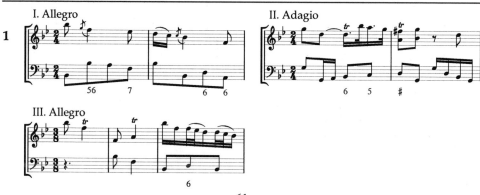

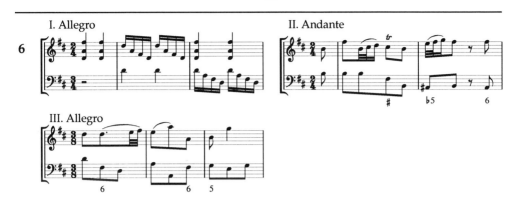

17   SONATAS FOR 2 GERMAN FLUTES

Opus 14, London, 1747
3 sonatas for 2 flutes
(A e A)

EARLY EDITION

JOHN WALSH, London, [1747]
Score, octavo, engraved, pagination explained below.

| HASSE | &c. | Select Duets | For two | GERMAN FLUTES | or | VIOLINS | Call'd | The Delightfull Musical Companion. | VOL. I [part 3d. ms] | London. Printed for I. Walsh, in Catharine Street, in | the Strand. Just Publish'd, | Handel's Select Aires and Duets for 2 German Flutes in 4 Books | Teleman's Duets. Locatelli's Duets. Forest Harmony, 4 Books | for 2 German Flutes or French Horns. Loeillet and Valentine's Sonatas for 2 German Flutes.|

EXEMPLAR: British Library d. 139.
DATING: Walsh II #553.
OTHER EXTANT COPIES: **GB** Gm(incomplete), Lcm (incomplete), Oc.
CITATIONS: RISM B II,199; BUCEM I,452; BMCPM I,602.
NOTE: Valentine pieces are found as follows: v.1 pt.3--"Duet or Sonata VII" pp.61-66, "Duet or Sonata VIII" pp.67-72; v.1 pt.4--"Duet or Sonata   IX" pp.73-77. (p.61 bottom rh corner "Valentine O:14"; p.67 bottom lh corner Valentine Op:14"; p.73 bottom lh corner "Valentini Op".14".) (Note on exemplar)

MODERN EDITION

Drei Sonaten für zwei Flöten, op. 14, Wilhelmshaven: Pegasus-ausgabe; New York: C.F. Peters Corp., c1972. (Arte del flauto).--N 1341.

NOTES: Edited from a printed copy in the British Library.

18 SONATE

à due oboè
1719?
12 sonatas and a pastorale for 2 oboes
(C C G C G F G G C C a G G)

MANUSCRIPT

British Library. Additional Ms. #38531. f. 1-37.
Sonate à due oboè, <u>In</u> Musica del Signore Roberto Valentine Inglese.
Ms. score, oblong quarto, 47 leaves

CITATION: Willetts, 4.

19   SONATE

à due oboe sù l'aria di tromba
1719?
18 arias for 2 oboes
(C C C C C C C C C C C C C C C C C C)

MANUSCRIPT

British Library. Additional Ms. 38531. f. 39-46.
Sonate à due oboe sù l'aria di tromba, In Musica del Signore Roberto Valentine Inglese.
Ms. score, oblong quarto, 47 leaves.

CITATION: Willetts, 4.
NOTE: f.46 also bears pagination "47".

MODERN EDITION

18 leichte Stücke für 2 Trompeten; Hrsg. von Frank Nagel.--Mainz: B. Schott's Söhne, c1970.
(Edition Schott, 6169).

NOTES: Edited from Additional Ms. 38531 in the British Library.

SOUND RECORDING

[Selections]

In   Europäische Barockmusik für Trompete und Orgel.--RBM Musikproduktion, [1979?].--3 026.
Klaus E. Rehm, Edward H. Tarr, trumpets.

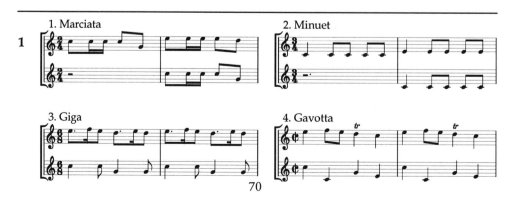

70

20 SONATE

d'oboè con il basso
1719?
12 sonatas for oboe with continuo
(F C G a g C B♭ G d F a C)

MANUSCRIPTS

Library of Congress. M242.V Case. f. 1-47.
Sonate à flauto traversiro [sic] solo con il basso, del Sig^r Roberto Valentini Inglese, in Roma.
Ms. score, oblong quarto (21 x 28 cm.), 47 leaves.

NOTE: ca. 1750 on inside front cover.
CITATION: NUC MBMSR 1958-62, 1016.

British Library. Additional Ms. 38531. f. 48-93.
Sonate d'oboè con il basso. In Musica del Signore Roberto Valentine Inglese.
Ms. score, oblong quarto, 47 leaves.

CITATION: Willetts, 4.
NOTE: f. 49 also bears pagination "48".

MODERN EDITIONS

[No. 1]

Sonata no. 1 in F, for oboe and piano; [Leonard] Lefkovitch [and Walter] Bergmann, ed.--London: Schott [c1952]. (Edition Schott 10097).

[No. 8]

Sonata no. 8 in G, for oboe and piano; [Leonard] Lefkovitch [and Walter] Bergmann, ed.--London: Schott [c1952]. (Edition Schott 10097).

SOUND RECORDINGS

[No. 1]

In   Blockflöte und Oboe im europaïschen Barock.--Pelca, [1979?].--PSR 40 618.
Peter Jenne, recorder; Dieter Leicht, violoncello; Heiner Rühner, harpsichord.

In   Trompete und Orgel.--Mixtur Schallplatten, [1979?].--VG 30 112.
Paul Falentin, trumpet; Bernard Heiniger, organ.

[No.8]

In   Rene Clemencic.--Harmonia Mundi, [1979?].--F 384.
Rene Clemencic, recorder.

In   Weihnachtliche Musik des Barock.--Calig Verlag, [1979?].--CAL 30 503. Kurt Hausmann,
oboe; Berthold Hummel, violoncello; Günther Lena, harpsichord.

21   SONATE

à due violoncelli
1719?
6 sonatas for violoncello with continuo
(C G a B♭ D F)

MANUSCRIPT

British Library. Additional Ms. 54207.
Sonate à due violoncelli del Sig^r: Roberto Valentini Inglese.
Ms. score, oblong quarto, 13 leaves.

CITATION: Willetts, 68.

22   CONCERTI GROSSI

6 concerti grossi for 2 violins with continuo
(D B♭ F C G A)

MANUSCRIPT

Uppsala. Universitätsbibliotheket. I Mhs. 61.2 a-f.
Violino del concerto grosso da Roberto Valentine Inglese a Roma.
6 ms. parts, oblong folio:
violino primo 25 p., violino secondo 25 p., basso 25 p.,
violino primo del concertino 25 p., violino secondo del concertino 25 p., basso del concertino 25 p.

CITATION: Eitner X, 25.

79

23 SONATA SECONDA

Concerto in B♭ major for recorder with strings
(B♭)

MANUSCRIPT

Naples. Conservatorio di S. Pietro a Majella. Biblioteca.38.3.13.
Sonata seconda. In Concerti di Flauto, Violini, Violetta, Basso, di diversi autori.
5 ms. parts, oblong folio:
flauto f.4-5; violino primo f.54-56; violino secondo f.104-106; violoncello f.162-163; basso f.212-213.

CITATION: Gasperini (Naples),548. Facsimile.

MODERN EDITION

Concerto B-Dur für Altblockflöte, 2 Violinen und Basso continuo; Hrsg. von Reinhard
Goebel.--Mainz; London: Schott. 1980. (Antiqua; eine Sammlung alter Musik.--ANT 139).

SOUND RECORDING

In Concerti per flauto.--Archiv Produktion, p1978.--2533 380.
Gudrun Heyens, recorder; Musica Antiqua Köln.

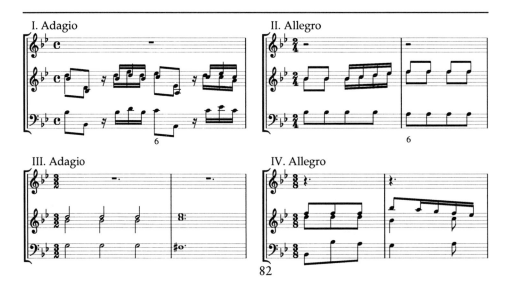

24 SONATA

con flauto traversiero ô oboè
Concerto for flute with strings
(D)

MANUSCRIPT

Rostock. Universitätsbibliothek. Mus. saec. XVIII 61².
Sonata con flauto traversiero ô oboè, violini, violette,
violone è cimbalo, violoncello, del Sign: Valentini.
6 ms. parts:
violoncello [1 p.]; flauto traversiero ô oboè [3 p.]; violino primo [3 p.];
violino secondo [3 p.]; violetta [3 p.]; [Bc] [2 p.].

CITATION: Eitner X,26.
NOTE: Title from cover.

MODERN EDITION

Concerto in D major, for flute or oboe, strings, and continuo. Percy Young, ed.--London: Chappell,
1967.

NOTE: edited from copyist's ms. in the Library of the University of Rostock.

SOUND RECORDING

In   Europäiches Barock-Konzert.--Philips, [1979?].--6701 011.
Zdenek Bruderhans, flute; Helmut Winschermann, conductor; Dt. Bachsolisten.

ARRANGEMENTS

25   SIX SONATAS OF TWO PARTS

made on purpose for two flutes
Opus 4, London, 1715
6 sonatas for two recorders
(C D F G C D)

NOTE: Arrangement of 5. *Six Sonatas.*
Several of the editions described below were issued originally as parts
of sets that correspond to the same editions listed in 26. *Six Sonatas
of Two Parts.* Indications of these relationships are noted when
necessary.

EARLY EDITIONS

[Nos. 1, 2, 4, & 5]

SINE NOMINE, s.l., s.d.
Score, oblong octavo, 25 p.

| [cartouche] | Divertimento | a due Flauti | Dedicato | All'Altezza R^{lc}. | DI GIO: GASTONE | Gran
Principe di Toscana | da Roberto Valentine Inglese | Opera Sesta |

EXEMPLAR: Biblioteca nazionale centrale, Florence. Mus.St.162.
OTHER EXTANT COPIES: D MÜs, I Ac
CITATIONS: RISM AI V70; Sartori,124.
NOTE: See 26. *Six Sonatas of Two Parts* for further information.

JOHN WALSH / JOHN HARE, London, [1715]
2 parts, folio, engraved, violino primo 12 p., violino secondo 12 p.

| [frame] | Six | Sonata's | of two Parts | for | Two | Violins | Compos'd by | Mr. Valentine | at Rome
| Opera Quarta | [rule] | London Printed for I: Walsh Servt. in Ordinary to his Majesty at the | Harp
and Hoboy in Catherine Street in the Strand, and I: Hare at the | Viol and Flute in Cornhill near the
Royall Exchange. |

EXEMPLAR: British Library h. 11. e.

DATING: Walsh I,480.
OTHER EXTANT COPIES: **GB** Olc--**US** CA, CHu, Su, Wc.
CITATIONS: RISM AI V59; BUCEM II,1032; BMCPM II,614; Walsh I #480; Wood,1519.

JOHN WALSH / JOHN HARE, London, [1715]
2 parts, folio, engraved, flauto primo 12 p., flauto secondo 12 p.

| [frame] | Six | SONATA'S | of two Parts | made on purpose | for two FLUTES | Compos'd by | Mr: Valentine | at Rome | Opera Quarta | [rule] | London Printed for I: Walsh Servt. in Ordinary to his Majesty at the | Harp and Hoboy in Catherine Street in the Strand, and I: Hare at the | Viol and Flute in Cornhill near the Royall Exchange. |

EXEMPLAR: British Library h. 11. d.
DATING: Walsh I #468.
OTHER EXTANT COPIES: **GB** CDp, Olc--**US** Wc (flute II only).
CITATIONS: RISM AI V61; BUCEM II,1032; BMCPM II,614; Walsh I #468.

[Nos. 1, 2, 4, & 5]

HOTTETERRE / BOIVIN, Paris, 1721.
Score, oblong folio, engraved, 39 p.

| [frame] | Sonates a Deux Dessus | Par le Sig^r. | Roberto Valentine | Opera Quinta. | accomodées a la Flûte Traversiere par M^r. Hotteterre le Rom^n. | Ordinaire de la Musique de la chambre du Roy. | Et se peuvent executer sur les autres Instrumens de Dessus. | [short rule] | A Paris Prix. 3^{lt} to l broché | Chez Led^t. S^r. Hotteterre rue de Seine a L'Hotel d'Arras | le S^r. Boivin M^d. rue Saint Honore a la regle d'or| 1721. |

DEDICATION

| Loüis, par la grace de Dieu, Roy de France et de Navarre, a nos ames il jeaux Consed^{re}. | les gens tenans nos Cours de Parlement, Maîtres des Requêtes ordinaires de Notre hôtel, Gr^d. Cons^t. | Prevost de Paris, Baillifs, Senechaux, leurs Lieutenans civils, et autres nos Justiciers qu'il apparliêdra, | Salut. Notre bien ame * * nous ayant fait suplier de luy accorder nos lettres de Permission pour faire | gravier ou imprimer les Sonates pour les Flûtes traversieres et autres Instrum^s. de la composition de Rober | to Valentine, Nous avons permis et permel^s. par ces presentes aud^t. Expos^t. de faire graver ou imprim^r. les Sonates | cy dess^s. expliquées, en telle forme, marge, caractere, en un ou plusieurs volumes, conjointem^t. ou separem^t. et autt. | de fois que bon luy semblera, et de les faire vendre et debiter par tout notre Royaume pend_t. le temps de trois | années consecutives a compter du jour de la date desdites presentes. Faisons deffences a tous grav^{rs}. imprim^{rs}. | libraires, marchands en taille douce, et autres de quela; qualité et condition qu'ils soient d'en introduire | d'impression etrangere dans aueun lieu de notre obeissance; a la charge que ces presentes seront enregistrées | tout au long sur le registre de la communauté des libraires et imprimeurs de Paris, et ce dans trois mois | de la date d'icelles; que la gravûre et impression desdites Sonates sera faite dans notre Royaume et | non ailleurs, en bon papier et en beaux caracteres conformément aux reglemens de la librairie, Et | qu'avant que de les exposer en vente les manuscrits, ou imprimès, ou gravés qui auront servy de copie a | la gravûre ou impression desdites Sonates cy dessus specifiées seront remis és mains de notre tres cher | et feal chevalier Chancelier de France le Sieur Daguesseau, et qu'il en sera ensuitte mis deux Exemplat | res dans notre biblioteque publique, un dans celle de notre Château du Louvre, et un dans celle de red^t. | tres cher et feal Chevalier Chancelier de France le Sieur Daguesseau, le tout a peine de nullité des | presentes Du conteau desquelles vous mandons et enjoign^s. de faire jouir ledit expos^t. ou ses ayant | cause pleinem^t. et paisiblem^t. sans souffrir qu'il leur soit fait aucun trouble ou empechemens. Voulons | qu'a la copie des presentes qui sera imprimée ou gravée tout au long au comencem^t. ou a la fin desidita | Sonates foy soit adjoutée comme a l'original. Commandons au prem^r. notre hussier ou Sergent de | faire pour l'execution d'icelles tous actes requis et necessaires sans demander autre permission, et | nonobstant dameur de haro, charte normande, et lettres a ce contraires, Cartel est notre plaisir. | Donné a Paris le 24e. avril l'an de grace 1721. et de notre Regne

le Sixiéme. | Parle Roy en Son Conseil, Signe Carpol. [last line centered on page] |

> EXEMPLAR: Bibliothèque nationale VM⁷6501.
> OTHER EXTANT COPIES: F AG, Pc (2 copies).
> CITATIONS: RISM AI V66.
> NOTE: See 26. *Six Sonatas of Two Parts* for further information.

JOHN WALSH, London, [1730]

2 parts, folio, engraved, violino primo 12 p., violino secondo 12 p. Publisher's no. 442.

| [frame] | Six | Sonata's | of two Parts | for | Two | Violins | Compos'd by | Mr. Valentine | at Rome | Opera Quartᵃ. | [rule] | London Printed for I: Walsh Servt. in Ordinary to his Majesty at the Harp and Houboy in Catherine Street in the Strand | No. 442 |

> EXEMPLAR: British Library h. 11. i
> DATING: Walsh II #1484.
> OTHER EXTANT COPIES: US PHu.
> CITATIONS: RISM AI V60; BUCEM II,1032; BMCPM II,614; Walsh II #1484.

JOHN WALSH, London, [1730]

2 parts, folio, engraved, flauto primo 12 p., flauto secondo 12 p. Publisher's no. 58.

| [frame] | Six | SONATA'S | of two Parts | made on purpose | for two FLUTES | Compos'd by | Mᶠ: Valentine | at Rome | Opera Quarta | [rule] | London Printed for I: Walsh Servᵗ. in Ordinary to his Majesty at the Harp and Houboy in Catherine Street in the Strand | Nᵒ. 58 |

> EXEMPLAR: British Library h.11.(9.)
> DATING: Walsh II #1483.
> OTHER EXTANT COPY: I BGi
> NOTICES: Oct. 6-8, 1715, *Post Man* (for earlier printing of the same edition) (Walsh II #1483).
> CITATIONS: RISM AI V62; BUCEM II,1032; BMCPM II,614; Walsh II #1483.

MODERN EDITIONS

[Nos. 1, 2, 4, & 5]

Sei sonate per due flauti dolci contralto;
ed. by Elio Peruzzi.--Padova: G. Zanibon, c1973 (G. 5295 Z.).

> NOTE: See 26. *Six Sonatas of Two Parts* for further information.

[Nos. 4 & 5]

Sechs Sonaten für zwei Alt-Blackflöten in f', Querflöten oder Violinen;
hrsg. von Hildemarie Peter.--Berlin-Lichterfelde: R. Lienau (vormals Schlesinger), c1957.
(Zusammenspiel für Blockflöten).

> NOTE: See 26. *Six Sonatas of Two Parts* for further information.

26   SIX SONATAS OF TWO PARTS

for two flutes
Opus 6, London, c.1720
6 sonatas for two recorders
(d F C a g E♭)

NOTE: Arrangement of 7. *Six Sonatas.*
Several of the editions described below were issued originally as parts
of sets that correspond to the same editions listed in 25. *Six Sonatas
of Two Parts.* Indications of these relationships are noted when
necessary.

EARLY EDITIONS

[Nos. 3 & 6]

SINE NOMINE, s.l., s.d.

See 25. *Six Sonatas of Two Parts* for description.

NOTE: No. 6 transposed to F major.

JOHN WALSH / JOHN HARE, London, [1720]
2 parts, folio, engraved, flauto primo 11 p., flauto secondo 11 p.

| [frame] | Six | SONATAS | of two Parts | for two | FLUTES | Compos'd by | Mr: Valentine | at
Rome | Opera 6ta. [6ta. in ms.] | [rule] | London Printed for I: Walsh Servt. in Ordinary to his
Majesty at the | Harp and Hoboy in Catherine Street in the Strand, and I: Hare at the | Viol and
Flute in Cornhill near the Royall Exchange. |

EXEMPLAR: Library of Congress ML30.4c no. 2133 Miller
DATING: Walsh I #572.
CITATIONS: RISM AI V69; Walsh I #572.

[Nos. 3 & 6]

HOTTETERRE / BOIVIN, Paris, 1721

See 25. *Six Sonatas of Two Parts* for description.

NOTE: No. 6 transposed to F major.

JOHN WALSH, London, [1730]

2 parts, folio, engraved, flauto primo 11 p., flauto secondo 11 p. Publisher's no.61.

| [frame] | Six | SONATAS | of two Parts | for two | FLUTES | Compos'd by | M^r: Valentine | at Rome | Opera 6ta. | [rule] | London Printed for I: Walsh Servt. in Ordinary to his Majesty at the Harp & Hoboy | in Catherine Street in the Strand | N°. 61 |

EXEMPLAR: British Library g. 71 f. (7).
DATING: Walsh II #1486.
CITATIONS: RISM AI V68; BUCEM II,1032; BMCPM II,614; Walsh II #1486.

MODERN EDITIONS

[Nos. 1,2,3 & 4]

Four sonatas for two flutes, David Glazer, ed.--New York: C. Fischer, c1951.

[Nos. 1,2,3 & 4]

Vier Duette für Altblockflöten (Querflöten, Oboen, Violinen) aus op. VI, Hrsg. von Hugo Ruf.--Mainz: B. Schott's Söhne; New York: Schott Music Corp., c1969. (Edition Schott, 5741).

[Nos. 1,3,5, & 6]

Sechs Sonaten; See 25. *Six Sonatas of Two Parts* for description.

[Nos. 3 & 6]

Sei Sonate; See 25. *Six Sonatas of Two Parts* for description.

NOTE: No. 6 transposed to F major.

6

FRAGMENTS

27 SIX SONATAS OF TWO PARTS

for two flutes
Opus 8, London, 171-
6 sonatas for two recorders
(D F C G d C)

EARLY EDITIONS

RICHARD MEARES, London, s.d.
Score, folio, engraved, fluto primo, 7 p.

I Six I Sonatas I in two Parts I for two I FLUTES. I Compos'd by I M^r: Valentine I at Rome I Opera 8 I [rule] I LONDON, I Printed for Richard Meares Musical Instrument Maker and Musick Printer, at the Golden Viol & Hautboy in S^t. Pauls Church Yard. I

EXEMPLAR: Library of Congress ML 30.4c no. 2134 Miller.
CITATIONS: RISM AI V75; NUC MBMSR 1968-72, III, 600.
NOTE: 1st flute only.

J. Bradford Young is Music Technical Services Librarian of the Otto E. Albrecht Music Library at the University of Pennsylvania in Philadelphia. He has studied and worked in music cataloging, and is involved in efforts for the bibliographic control of music through the Music Library Association and the American Library Association.